SERMONS ON
NEW TESTAMENT CHARACTERS

Rev. CLOVIS G. CHAPPELL, D.D.

SERMONS ON NEW TESTAMENT CHARACTERS

BY

REV. CLOVIS G. CHAPPELL, D.D.

Author of "The Village Tragedy," "Sermons on Biblical Characters," "More Sermons on Biblical Characters," "The Modern Dance," etc.

NEW YORK

GEORGE H. DORAN COMPANY

SERMONS ON NEW TESTAMENT CHARACTERS
— B —
PRINTED IN THE UNITED STATES OF AMERICA

CONTENTS

SERMONS ON
NEW TESTAMENT CHARACTERS

SERMONS ON NEW TESTAMENT CHARACTERS

I

THE LARGEST GIVER—THE POOR WIDOW

Mark 12 : 43

> "Verily I say unto you, that this poor widow
> hath cast more in, than all they which have
> cast into the treasury."

I

The scene is the Temple of God in Jerusalem. The collection is being taken. Christ is present and is watching the proceedings with keen interest. He always does. He is profoundly concerned with what we do with our money. He is ever attentive to our financial programmes. He is abidingly interested in our conduct when the offering is taken. He watches with deep concern what we do when we face the collection plate.

Church people sometimes say: "I wish my pastor would preach the Gospel and stop talking about money." But it is impossible to preach the Gospel and not talk about money. Christ had more to say about money than He had to say about repentance, as vital as that subject is. He had more to say about money than He had to say about the new birth. He had more to say about money than He had to say about heaven. He had more to say about money than He had to say about hell. It is impossible, therefore, to preach the Gospel and not deal with this vital subject of money.

1. Christ is interested in the collection because money is power. Money is pent up force. It can be used for the defeating of the ends of justice. It can be used for the wrecking of character. It can be used for the retarding of the progress of the Kingdom of God. It can also be used for the promotion of that Kingdom. It can be used for the purifying of society and for the rebuilding of shattered and broken lives. Christ is therefore naturally profoundly interested in what we do with whatever financial power comes into our possession.

2. Christ is interested in the collection because what we do with our money is an index to our characters. The man who invests largely in the pursuit of pleasure is a pleasure seeker. The man who invests largely in books is a lover of literature. The man who invests largely in the Church of Jesus Christ is quite likely to be a Christian. Of course a man may give and give liberally and yet not be a saint. But it is utterly impossible to be a saint and be niggardly and stingy in our giving. What a man does with his money is a good indication of what he is.

For this reason every collection is a kind of judgment occasion. For this reason the plate that receives your offering becomes a throne before which your character is tested. You judge yourself. If the opportunity to give is an offence to you, if you are bored by it, if you are annoyed and even at times angered, you mark yourself not as an unselfish lover of Jesus Christ, but as a selfish lover of the world. If, on the other hand, you rejoice in the privilege of giving, you mark yourself as kindred to your Lord, whose supreme task is giving from eternity to eternity.

Not only do we judge ourselves in the presence of the collection plate, but Christ also judges us. He cannot help it. He sees what we give. If our gifts are mean and niggardly, He knows it. If they are sweet with the sacrificial breath of Calvary, He knows that. Therefore, when we face the collection plate, we either sadden our Lord or we gladden Him. We win His approval or His disapproval. We call forth either His commendation or His condemnation. We judge ourselves and are judged by our Lord by what we do with the wealth that He has put into our hands.

II

What did Jesus see as He sat over against the treasury?

1. He saw much that was commendable. He saw many rich men cast their gifts into the treasury. That was fine. There were rich men in that far-off day that were interested in the Church of God. They were interested enough to attend it. They were interested enough to support it by their means. And, thank God, there are such still. All the wealth is not in the hands of the Godless. There are rich men who are not too tired on Sunday morning to come to God's house. They do not all have to rest by going to the golf links and desecrating the Sabbath Day. Many of them are found in the Church and many of them give of their means to the support of the Church.

2. Not only were the rich men present with their

gifts that day, but they were liberal in their giving. "Many that were rich cast in much." These rich men did not give meanly. They did not say: "I will give my mite." Many a stingy man has read this story and has found in it only an excuse for increased stinginess. For a rich man to have given a mite would have been nothing less than a burning shame. These men did not throw in pennies when they might have thrown in dollars. They gave liberally. "Many that were rich cast in much." It was a magnificent offering that was made for the Lord's cause on that day.

3. But there was one giver who did not cast in much. "There came a certain poor widow." She was a woman who had suffered. She was a woman who had had her heart broken. She was a woman who had known the pinch of poverty. Not only had she known what it was to be miserably poor, but that was a present experience with her. She felt no uneasiness lest her home should be burglarised while she was at church. There was not the fraction of a penny in her humble little home. All she had in the world was in her hand. And that was so little that she was half ashamed to give it. And yet she could not withhold it. And so she cast into the treasury two mites, which make a farthing.

Had you been by when this money was counted at the close of the day, you would not have heard any praise for the great gift of this widow. It was only a fraction of a cent. It was hardly worth counting. But the many gifts of those who gave much bulked large. Any adding machine could have added them, but there was that in the gift of the widow that was beyond the power of the best adding machine. Christ alone could rightly estimate the full value of it. And when He had cast up the amount, He declared, "This poor widow hath cast more in than all they which have cast into the treasury."

III

What was there in this gift of the widow that made it more than all the gifts that the rich cast into the treasury? Certainly it was not more in amount.

1. It was more because it represented more fidelity on the part of the giver. It was so little that this widow could give. "What are two mites worth toward the carrying on of God's work in the world?" she might have asked. "What are they worth to Him who holds the wealth of the world in His hands? They will mean next to nothing to Him. They mean much to me. They are all I have." The human thing, therefore, for her to have done was simply to have done nothing. How many take that position! Their name is legion. But what lies back of such conduct? Unfaithfulness. And the one who is unfaithful in the least will also be unfaithful in much. It is not a question of how much good your gift will do to the cause of God. It is a question rather of your fidelity in the handling of that gift for your Lord, however small it may be.

A young fellow beat the street car conductor out of his car fare in our city the other day. What said he in excuse for his dishonesty? This: "The street car company is a large corporation. It has ample means. It certainly will not miss the seven cents that I failed to pay it. It does not need an amount so insignificant." But that is not the question. The street car company can get on without his seven cents, but he cannot get on well without being honest. The tragedy is not that the street car company will go broke without his money. It is rather that he will go morally broke by failing to be square. And it is not the fact that Jesus Christ cannot carry on His work in the world without our small gifts that constitutes the calamity of our failure to give. It is rather that we cannot otherwise hope to win His approval and enable Him to say: "Ye have been faithful over a few things, I will make you ruler over many things."

Fidelity in the use of our gifts and in the use of our means, however small, this is what wins the approval of our Lord. And this widow was bent on being faithful. She did not give simply because she felt like it. She gave because it was her duty to give. She gave because it was right. And, my brethren, we shall never give so as to meet the divine approval until we give from conviction. Some church members are liberal under the pastorate of one man and stingy under the pastorate of another. Such givers receive no commendation from Jesus Christ. He rather approves those that give from principle. He commends those who, whatever the situation is, are faithful in whatever talents He has put into their hands. It took a vast amount of fidelity to cause this widow to give this meagre gift, far more than was required of the rich to give their larger gifts.

2. This widow cast in more than all the rest in that her gift was more expensive to herself. There was more sacrifice in what she did. These rich men gave liberally, but they did not give sacrificially. They gave of their abundance. They gave of their superfluity. They did not have to deny themselves of a single pleasure because of what they gave. They did not have less to eat nor less to wear nor less comfortable homes in which to live. Their gifts were large, but they were not stained

by blood nor soaked in sweat. They only gave what they did not really need for themselves.

But the gift of the widow was costly. It cost her everything. When those two mites slipped from her lean fingers, she had absolutely nothing left. Her gift was, therefore, shot through with the spirit of the Cross. If there is no sacrifice in our service, if there is no sacrifice in our giving, then it is not Christian. Costless giving may help after a fashion, but it is not beautiful either in the eyes of God or of men. Christ puts His stamp of approval only on the giving that costs. His gifts cost Him something. Ours are to cost us something.

There is an old story of an artist who painted a picture that was touched by a lovely and fascinating crimson that no other artist was able to imitate. They studied this picture and sought for its secret in vain. But when the artist was dead and they were preparing him for burial, they noticed above his heart a half-healed wound. Then it was that they understood. As this artist had painted he had dipped his brush into his own heart's blood. That was the secret of the winsome crimson they could not imitate. That was the secret of the fascinating picture that had cast its spell upon them. They could not paint as he painted because they were unwilling to pay the price he paid. The picture that is beautiful is costly. And the giving that is beautiful is also costly.

3. This widow gave more than all the rest because there was more love in her giving. Her sacrifice would have gone for nothing had there been no love in it. "Though I bestow all my goods to feed the poor, and though I give my body to be burned, and have not love, it profiteth me nothing." The richest of gifts are but so

much refuse in the sight of God if there is a sordid motive behind them. On the other hand, the smallest gift is beautiful beyond all words if it is given for love's sake.

This widow gave because she loved. She was not seeking popular applause. She knew she would not find it. She was giving because her love would not allow her to withhold. For love, you know, is very active. It is very insistent upon doing something. It will do the big thing if it can. If it cannot, it will do the little thing. It will adorn a palace if it can. If it cannot, it will beautify and sweeten a cabin. It will serve in a big way if it is within its power. If not, it will serve in an obscure and hidden way. But of this you may be sure, love will give and give of its best. And that best will make the strongest possible appeal to the heart of Christ. It will also make the strongest appeal to the hearts of men.

Some years ago a saintly woman of my acquaintance told me of a visit she made to a sick girl away back in the heart of the hills. The girl's father was little more than an outcast. Her mother was dead. There she lay upon a bed that had no sheets. Her head was upon pillows that had no coverings. She seemed absolutely destitute of all knowledge of Christ. Into that needy home this women went and out of her own poverty she ministered, and to this benighted girl who was dying of consumption she preached Jesus. At her last visit the girl said: "I will not be living when you come again. Here is a keepsake I want to give you to remember me by." And she gave the woman who had led her to Christ a little pin that was not worth five cents anywhere. Yet it was the best she had. And that pin is a treasure to that saintly woman to-day. Love's tears had fallen upon it and had been transformed into diamonds. She values it because it is the best gift of a grateful and loving heart.

IV

Now, since this poor widow made the largest gift that was brought to the treasury that day, her story is one full of encouragement for ourselves.

1. It heartens us because it puts the very poorest of us on an equal footing with the richest. We who have the smallest gifts have exactly the same opportunity of winning God's approval as those who have the largest. Who will be the largest contributor to First Methodist Church this year? We do not know. It may be the one who has more wealth than any other man in the church. It may be the one who has the least. It will surely be the one who is most faithful and most sacrificing and most loving in the doing of what he can. The one who does that will rank with this poor widow. He will be graded as she was, one hundred per cent. The richest man in all the world cannot pass that mark. But the poorest in all the world can reach to it.

2. This story heartens us because it tells us the very smallest gifts, if they are our best, are not despised. Men may despise them. Sometimes they do. But this is true only when they fail to understand. Our Lord never fails to understand. Therefore, He never looks upon them with contempt. If two mites are our best, His heart glows with gladness just as much as if we had given millions. And if it be so that we have not even that much, He will receive with gladness whatever we give. "He that giveth a cup of cold water shall not lose his reward."

Therefore, since God does not despise our gifts, however small, let us see to it that nothing prevents us from offering them. Let us not be prevented from doing so by self-pity. Let not the pity of others prevent us. When we made the every member canvass a few weeks ago, some returned saying that they went into homes that were so poor that they hesitated to accept an offering. But let us not become pitiful beyond our Lord. He had no hesitancy in accepting the last mite from this poor widow. He will take the last penny you have and He will do it joyfully.

But this He will do not because He is grasping. He will do it because He knows that it is more blessed to give than to receive. He will do it because He knows our giving conditions our receiving. "Give, and it shall be given unto you." The sureness of your giving conditions the sureness of your receiving. A hand that is wide open to give will be wide open to receive. The hand that recklessly gives all will receive all. Therefore our Lord does not hesitate to take our very last mite because such giving does not impoverish us, but makes us rich forevermore. Let us therefore aspire to the place of the largest giver, for in so doing we will also win the place of the largest receiver.

II

THE EVANGELIST—PHILIP

The Acts 8 : 35

"Then Philip opened his mouth, and began
at the same scripture, and preached unto him
Jesus."

I

"Then Philip opened his mouth." That is fine.
That is exceedingly hopeful. One of the tragedies of
many who are in the Church to-day is that of the closed
mouth. So many seem possessed with the demon of
dumbness. We open our mouths to eat. We open our
mouths to buy and sell. We open our mouths to gossip.
We sometimes open our mouths to criticise. But too
few of us open our mouths to preach Jesus.

"Then Philip opened his mouth." That indicates
courage. It is only a few days since Philip has seen a
very ugly murder that was committed because a certain
friend of his insisted upon opening his mouth. If
young Stephen of the clear head and shining face and
Spirit-filled heart had only kept silent, he would not
have been mobbed. If he had only known how to hold
his tongue, he would not have been the victim of those
cruel stones. If he had not insisted upon opening his
mouth, his mangled body would not now be lying in its
untimely grave up Jerusalem way. He was determined
to open his mouth and proclaim the good tidings of
great joy. Hence he died a martyr.

19

Philip was well aware of all these facts.   Therefore, as he fled from Jerusalem, Prudence walked at his
side with her wise counsel and said: "Now, Philip, it is
all right to be a Christian; it is well enough to be a follower of Jesus Christ, but do not be too outspoken.   Do
not insist on telling your story to others.   Learn to keep
silent."   But in spite of all these very sane admonitions,
it stands written in the text that "Philip opened his
mouth."   It was a courageous thing to do.   It is a thing
that many of us are afraid to do to this day.   We are
not afraid to talk on many themes, but to open our
mouth to preach Jesus is something the very thought
of which fills us with a kind of terror.

"Then Philip opened his mouth."   That speaks also
of spontaneity.   Philip was not simply driving himself
to preach.   He felt that he could not help speaking.   His
testimony would have been that of some of his fellow-
disciples: "We cannot but speak the things that we have
seen and heard."   There was good news in his heart that
was clamouring for utterance.   There were Niagaras of
Gospel truth beating against the gateway of his lips and
demanding an outlet.   So full was this man of his joyous theme that preaching Jesus was not so much a duty
as a privilege.   "Then Philip opened his mouth, and
began at the same scripture, and preached unto him
Jesus."

II

Who was Philip?

He was not one of the apostles.   He was not an or-
dained minister.   Philip was a layman.   He was a member of the Official Board of the First Church of Jerusalem.   When the apostles decided that it was necessary

that seven men be elected to look after the temporal affairs of this infant church, Philip was one of the men chosen. He was not chosen for the work of the ministry primarily. He was chosen for the lowly task of serving tables. Yet we remember this man to-day not so much because he was a competent man of business as because he was a Spirit-filled and effective evangelist.

Philip conducted a successful revival in Samaria. He was used of God in preaching to the multitudes. But doubtless if you had talked to him near the end of his pilgrimage, he would have told you that the most useful part of his ministry had been his work with the individual. He would have said: "I have been able to render my largest service to my Master through my dealing with men face to face and heart to heart." If Philip had not so said, he would be an exception to the rule. For the most successful evangelists through all the years have won their greatest victories for the Kingdom through dealing with men one by one.

And this type of preaching is possible for every one of us. All of us cannot proclaim God's message from the pulpit. But there is not one but can preach Jesus to the individual. This is a high and holy privilege that is within reach of the least as well as of the greatest. There is absolutely no doubt but that Jesus Christ expects every follower of His to be a soul-winner. It may be that we do not expect so much of ourselves. Sad to say, a large part of the Church to-day leaves this supremely important task to the pastor and to a few faithful workers. But it is all wrong. Preaching Jesus to the individual is the privilege of every Christian.

Not only is this the privilege of every one who is a

follower of Christ, it is also his solemn responsibility. Because we can preach Christ, therefore we ought to preach Him. And because we ought to preach, we are by no means guiltless if we refuse to do so. "Woe is me if I preach not the Gospel." That word befits the lips of every saint just as much as it befit the lips of Saint Paul. Because we can preach, we must preach. "Every branch in me that beareth not fruit, He taketh away." Even a fruitless fig tree met the curse of eternal barrenness. This was the case in spite of the fact that Christ had not invested His blood in the redemption of that fig tree. But He has invested it in the redemption of ourselves. We cannot, therefore, be fruitless and guiltless at the same time. Because we can preach, we must preach. Such was the conviction of Philip. He took the command of his Master to preach the Gospel to every creature seriously.

III

But how was it that the Lord was able to use him for this particular preaching mission?

1. He could do so because Philip was obedient. He was open to Divine guidance. He had faith enough to obey God even when obedience looked foolish and ridiculous. Philip was engaged in a great revival in Samaria when the message came to him to leave this city with its populous streets and rejoicing multitudes. While the shouts of those being won to Christ were yet in his ears, he was ordered to set out for a desert country miles away. It looked like a very foolish thing to do. But Philip obeyed.

There are very few of us who are willing, with this evangelist and with Paul, to be fools for Christ's sake.

We are wofully afraid of making ourselves ridiculous.
Joshua was a man of the type of Philip. How the wise
must have laughed at him when they saw the absurd
tactics that he was using for the capturing of Jericho.
He was employing no battering ram. He was not shoot-
ing an arrow. He was not hurling a single spear. He
was just marching round the city blowing a ram's horn.
It certainly was a foolish and ridiculous thing to do,
at least in the eyes of men. But the significant part of
the story is that he captured the city. I have known
many a campaign conducted in a far more sane and
dignified fashion to fail of its objective altogether.
Blessed the man who has learned to obey God, for "Behold, to obey is better than sacrifice."

So Philip set out from Samaria and journeyed toward the south. He did not know exactly the purpose
of his journey, but he was sure that his Lord was not
sending him upon a fool's errand. Therefore, he trav-
elled with open eye and attentive ear. He was looking
for some way to be of service. There are those that
tell us how willing they are to be useful, but they never
find anything to do. But to those who are really willing, no day passes without its opportunity. Again and
again friends cross our path whom we might help if we
are only eager and watchful as was Philip.

After quite a long journey Philip reached the forks of
the road. He came into the highway that leads down
from Jerusalem to Gaza. It was a barren and unsightly country and seemed a most unlikely place for
God to send a man to preach. Philip wonders what it
all means, but he is not left long in doubt. Just up the
road yonder he sees a chariot coming surrounded by a
retinue of soldiers and servants. A great man is ap-
proaching. Of that much he is sure. And then the

Spirit spoke within his heart: "Go near and join thyself to this chariot."

Philip was doubtless astonished. It seemed a strange command. There were dozens of good reasons for his refusing to obey. Had we been by we would possibly have warned Philip after this fashion: "That man coming there is a perfect stranger to you. You never saw him before and will doubtless never see him again. Besides, he is a very prominent man. He is Secretary of the Treasury for the Kingdom of Ethiopia. He is a man of ability. He is a man of wealth and political power. Your Gospel is well enough for the poor. It is altogether a fit message for the down-and-out. But do not make yourself ridiculous by trying to preach to a man like this Ethiopian Statesman. His cup is already full. He will therefore not hear you. In trying to make him hear, you will only injure your cause and make yourself a laughing stock."

Now it is good to remember that this Gospel of ours is for the poor and for the unfortunate and for the outcast. But it is not for these only. It is also for the rich and for the powerful and for those who in the eyes of the world seem most favoured of fortune. It is for the down-and-out. It is also for the up-and-out and for all in between. Society has no greater tendency to become rotten at the bottom than it does at the top. I do not know but that we are in more danger of moral decay in America at the top than at the bottom. Our Gospel is therefore needed by all. "For all have sinned and come short of the glory of God."

That was true of this Ethiopian Statesman. In spite of his position, in spite of all that wealth had flung into his lap, he has more heart-hunger than he knows how to manage. His soul is thirsting for God, for the living

God. His Maker has so fashioned him that it is utterly impossible for him to find rest and peace and abiding satisfaction apart from Himself. He cannot be content with things. An Unseen Presence is with him as he rides that will not let him be content. The Spirit of God is there striving with him, wooing him, making him to loathe the thing that he is and to long for the better man that he may be. And that same spirit is speaking to our hearts to-day. We may stop our ears to His appeal, but He lovingly pursues us. He is present with us in our infancy before our mother's lips have kissed us. Through all our wandering ways He journeys with us, convicting us of sin, seeking patiently to lure us to those heights of holy fellowship that are within reach even of the weakest and of the worst.

What response did Philip make to the command of the Spirit? He obeyed. He refused to be frightened by the position of this Ethiopian. It is easier to preach to one who is at the rear of the procession than to one near the front. But our message is for all. So Philip listened only to the voice of his Lord. And we read of him this fine word: "Philip ran." Notice the eagerness of him, the earnestness, the whole-hearted enthusiasm. He ran. Oh, for more fleet-footed saints! We need them in the pulpit. We need them on the Official Board. We need them as Sunday School teachers. We need them throughout the entire membership of the Church. We are so slow. We go with such leaden feet about our tasks. Oh, that this sentence might be written about a growing number of us, "He ran."

Philip was enthusiastic and whole-hearted in his obedience. He ran fleet-footed on the errands of his Lord. And as he thus goes running toward the chariot, I dare say that he was praying earnestly that the Lord would give him an opening. He was planning how he might tactfully begin the conversation. And nothing requires greater tact than soul winning. Soon he is close enough to see that the great man is reading. That seems to make his task more difficult. Possibly he is reading some document of state and will refuse to be disturbed. But Philip does not hesitate. He presses bravely on.

2. Philip knew his Bible. Now the Evangelist is within hearing distance. This Ethiopian is reading aloud. And when Philip heard what he was reading, he had to hug his heart to keep it from leaping from his bosom. The words were entirely familiar to him. He had learned them in the Synagogue when he was a child. He had had them flooded with infinite light by the events of recent days. There was not another passage in all the Word of God that Philip would have been quite so glad to find this Ethiopian Statesman reading as the one he was reading, which was none other than the fifty-third chapter of Isaiah.

The stately words came to him on the desert air : "We all like sheep have gone astray; we have turned every one to his own way; and the Lord hath laid on Him the iniquity of us all. But He was wounded for our transgressions. He was bruised for our iniquities; the chastisement of our peace was upon Him; and with His stripes we are healed." "He was led as a lamb to the slaughter, and as a sheep before his shearers is dumb, so He openeth not His mouth." And Philip looked to see the light break upon the face of the Ethiopian, but there was no light there. There was only a frown of perplexity.

"Pardon me, but do you understand what you are reading?" And Philip's face was so radiant and so

eager that the great statesman felt at once that here
was one who knew. "No, I do not understand," he answered. "How can I except some man teach me."
Christ uses men for the salvation of other men. He
seems shut up to that method. If there is not "some
man" to teach, then the seeking soul will not be won.
A message must have a messenger. An evangel is of no
avail without an evangelist. "How can they hear without a preacher?"

3. He knew his Lord. Then this statesman who did
not understand invited Philip into his chariot. And I
can imagine that few men ever mounted a chariot more
rapidly or more eagerly than did this evangelist. And
they re-read this marvellous passage together. "He was
wounded for our transgressions. He was bruised for
our iniquities; the chastisement of our peace was upon
Him; and with His stripes we are healed." And the
Ethiopian is asking Philip a question. "Of whom is the
prophet speaking? Of himself or of some other?" In
other words: "Who is this that was wounded for our
transgressions. Who is this Lamb of God that taketh
away the sin of the world. Who is it that is able to
deal adequately with sin in your life and mine?"

Who indeed? Preacher, do you know? Sunday
School Teacher, do you know? Member of the Official
Board, do you know? Who is it that saves? Parents,
with your responsibility of training young lives for
God, do you know? When the blear-eyed outcast asks
this question, have you an answer? When the bright-
eyed, questioning child in your home asks it, can you
answer? Who is it that saves? Do you know? Not
as a theory, not as a tradition, but as a personal experience?

Philip knew. "And he began at the same scripture

and preached unto him Jesus." Would you not have
liked to hear the sermon? We can imagine how it ran.
"Of whom is the prophet speaking?" asked the Ethiopian. "He is not speaking of himself," the Evangelist
replies, "he is speaking of Jesus. He is speaking of
the One who was crucified in Jerusalem a few months
ago. He is speaking of Him who conquered death and
hell and the grave. He is speaking of One who is 'able
to save unto the uttermost them that come unto God by
Him.' He is our sin bearer. 'With His stripes we are
healed.' All you have to do is just to accept the healing
that He brings to you; receive the salvation that He
offers you."

And while Philip is yet speaking a light breaks upon
the darkened face of the African Statesman. He enters upon the blessed experience that, thank God, is for
all men in all times and in all climes. This man who
was on his way from church with his heart yet hungry
then and there found the Bread of Life. This man who,
in spite of the magnificent ritual of the Temple, was yet
burning with thirst, then and there "drank of the water
of life freely." And we read this happy ending of the
story: that he went on his way rejoicing. And not only
did he rejoice, but it is safe to say that many another
weary soul came to share his joy with him in the dark
continent of Africa.

This scene brings to my mind a football game that I
witnessed years ago. A husky fellow carrying the ball
for the opposing team broke through our line. He
dodged every antagonist. There is only one man now
between him and the goal. If he makes this goal, the
game is lost. And there is only one man to stop him,
our wiry little quarterback. How small he looks! He
seems not more than half the size of the man that is

carrying the ball. Can the quarterback stop him? That
was the question that made our hearts almost stand still.
If he cannot, then the game is lost.

The big husky bore down upon him. He made no
effort to dodge. He knew that his seemingly insignificant antagonist would be too quick for him. He rushed
into him head-on with the purpose of knocking him out.
Would the quarterback stand up to him? We knew that
if there was the least bit of yellow in him he would flinch
and lose. But he never gave an inch. And though I do
not know how it happened to this day, I do know this:
that even yet I can hear the terrific impact of the big
man's body against the ground where the little fellow
threw him. And the day was saved because this one
man, our last chance, stood in his place and held true.

And this, I am persuaded, was the last chance of the
Ethiopian. There was no man in Africa that knew
Jesus. He was leaving the saints of the early Church
long distances behind him. His one chance centres in
the Evangelist, Philip, and the Evangelist did not fail.
The battle was won and heaven was made glad, and the
heart of the saved and the heart of the preacher were
also made glad. And now the scene changes from that
far off day to this, and from that bit of desert country
to this populous city. And your road is running into
that of your friend, into that of your husband, into that
of your child. It is your opportunity to preach. It
is his opportunity to be saved. What are you going to
do about it?

IV

Now, let me remind you, my brethren, that it was
not simply by accident that this needy statesman and

this Spirit-guided Evangelist met that day at the forks
of the road. God's hand was in it. This Ethiopian
had been to Jerusalem. There were quite a few Christians there. But they had missed him in some way.
He had not been won by them. And now he is on his
way home. Unless somebody heads him off; unless
somebody hurries and gets between him and his destina-
tion, the chances are that he will never be reached. He
will go home and die without ever coming into possession of the Life that is life indeed. He will go home
with lips forever dumb that might have spoken a marvellous story to the glory of God and to the gladdening
of many saddened lives.

I dare to believe also that it is not by mere chance
that you and I have met at the forks of the road this
morning in God's house. You have come a long and
tedious journey. The preacher has also come a long
way to meet you. He did not dream years ago when he
entered the service of his Lord that his road would thus
cross yours. But here we are this morning, you and I,
at the forks of the road. I dare to believe that God has
put me in the path of some of you to keep you from
going away and missing the thrill of the knowledge of
Jesus Christ. I dare to believe that He has thrown
this message this Sabbath morning across your path
to keep some of you from the tragedy of a wasted life.

And will you not also dare to believe, my brethren,
that it is not merely by accident that your path has
crossed that of your friend? Will you not believe that
God has a blessed and holy purpose in bringing you into
intimate fellowship with the members of your own
household, with the pupils of your own class? You are
travelling as Christ's evangelist. Your road has run
into the road of a friend who is travelling away from

God.   The one big chance of that friend may be at your hands.   If you let him escape, he will never be reached. If you let your child slip by you unsaved, the chances are that he will spend his life in sin.   May God be able to write this about you, "He preached unto him Jesus."

THE DESERTER—DEMAS

II Timothy 4 : 10

"Demas hath forsaken me, having loved this
present world."

I

That is a disappointing sentence. It is the final
chapter in the story of this one time saint. Paul had
to write a word very much like this about John Mark
on one occasion. John Mark deserted Paul. But the
story of his desertion is not his final story. Mark came
back. "Take Mark and bring him with thee, for he is
profitable unto me for the ministry." That is the
last word we read about him. But Demas, so far as we
know, never came back. "Demas hath forsaken me."
He was gone when this pathetic sentence was penned,
and he remained gone to the end of the chapter.

"Demas hath forsaken me." What a tragic break-
down. But if this sentence tells of a disappointing
present, it also tells of a glorious past. It reminds us of
that good day in the life of Demas when he was the companion of Paul. It reminds us of that day when he was
the companion and fellow-worker of Paul's Lord.
Demas had shared the great hopes of this missionary
saint with whom he was associated. He participated in
his daring dreams. He had a part in his far and glori-

ous visions. Paul's purpose of world conquest was also in some measure the purpose of his friend, Demas.

Not only did this young man share in the daring dream of St. Paul, he also shared in his efforts toward the realisation of that dream. When Paul had gone forth to the preaching of the Gospel, Demas had walked at his side. When Paul had faced dangers, Demas had faced those dangers with him. When the foundation of a new church was laid, Demas was there. Demas had shared Paul's vision, and he had also shared Paul's task.

But that experience is of yesterday. That fascinating and heroic chapter is in the past. Demas is not found at the side of Paul any more. Demas no longer shares in Paul's dreams. He no longer labours at the high task that engaged his great-hearted friend. He has deserted his Master, Jesus Christ. And Paul writes with a sorrow that wets his face with tears. "Demas hath forsaken me."

II

What got the matter with Demas? Of what insidious disease did he sicken? Where began the little leak that set the waters to roaring about this pathetic wreck? Did Demas commit some crime that made it necessary for him to leave Rome? Did Demas get his hand into the coffers of the church and take that which was not his? Did Demas allow some ugly sin to grip him and squeeze the fine juices from his soul and fling him away into the Devil's garbage can?

No, Demas was guilty of no crime. He was besmirched by no disgraceful and ugly sin. The foe that wrought the ruin of Demas appears so innocent and harmless that we would scarcely regard it as a foe at all. What proved the undoing of Demas? The answer is in the text. "Demas hath forsaken me, having loved this present world."

So this text implies that if a man loves this present world he will cease to love God. It implies that the love of the world and the love of the Lord Jesus Christ cannot home in the same heart. And what is implied in this text is clearly taught elsewhere in the Word of God. John says: "Love not the world, neither the things that are in the world. If any man love the world, the love of the Father is not in him." He declares that the very moment the love of the world enters into our hearts, the love of God goes out. And James, if possible, makes it even more emphatic when he declares that the love of the world is enmity against God. That is, the lover of the world is not only not a lover of God, but he is God's personal enemy. And Paul wrote a letter one day that is bespattered with tears. He says: "I tell you even weeping that some of you are enemies of the cross of Christ." And that which made them enemies of the cross of Christ was that they minded earthly things. They were in love with the world.

Jesus Christ also spoke to the same purpose. He told Pilate frankly that His Kingdom was not of this world, that if His Kingdom were of this world, then would His servants fight. Those who were His children, those who were His subjects were not worldly. They were set free from the bondage of the love of the world. About the sharpest word that ever fell from His lips was that which He spoke to Peter when Peter urged Him to avoid the cross. "Be it far from thee, Lord," said this hot headed disciple when Jesus began to tell how He must suffer. But the Master was quick and cutting in His rebuke: "Get thee hence, Satan, for thou savourest not the things that be of God, but the things that be of men." That is, "You are not talking the language of the Godlike. You are talking the language of the world." So it is very evident that if the Bible is true we cannot love the world and be saints at the same time.

III

But what is this world that we are forbidden to love?

Surely it is not this physical universe of mountains and hills, of rivers and seas, of skies and stars. When God made these things He pronounced them very good. And if it should so happen that we admire them and even love them, I do not think for a moment that our Lord would object. Should we feel it in our hearts to exclaim:

"O world, as God has made it, all is beauty,
    And knowing this is love, and love is duty,"

I do not think that we would be talking in language that is unchristian. Were we to see in "the meanest flower that blows thoughts that often lie too deep for tears," I do not think that we would for that reason be displeasing to our Lord. Were we to find "sermons in stones, books in running brooks and good in everything," we would not thereby stamp ourselves as pagan. If we were to cry with Wordsworth, "Heaven lies about us in our infancy," and then pass on to the even finer strain of Lowell:

"Not only round our infancy
    Does heaven with all its splendour lie,

Daily with souls that cringe and plot,
We Sinais climb and know it not.
Over our manhood bend the skies,
Against our fallen and traitor lives
The great winds utter prophecy,
And to old age's drowsy blood
Still shouts the inspiring sea":

even here we would be talking the language of real
sainthood. When we are forbidden to love the world,
then, it is not that we are forbidden to love and admire
this beautiful physical world that God has given us.

Nor are we forbidden to love the world of men.
"God so loved the world that He gave His only begotten
Son." This love of God for the world was the love of
the men who live in the world. The more we love folks,
the more we become like Christ. Love is the big com-
modity that the world is short on:

"Do you know the world is dying
For a little bit of love?
Everywhere we hear them sighing
For a little bit of love.
For a love that rights the wrong,
Fills the heart with hope and song,
They have waited, oh, so long,
For a little bit of love."

No, we are certainly not forbidden to love the world of
men. Let yourself go in this matter of loving folks. A
broken-hearted mother said to me not long ago that she
was afraid she loved her first-born son too much. He
was a fine, clean young fellow, and he was lying down-
stairs in his coffin at that moment. When she said: "I
am afraid I loved him too much and God took him

away," I could but answer, "No, no, mother, you did not love him too much. You may have loved God too little. We all do that. But you did not love your laddie too much." The big tragedy of your life and mine is that we love so little.

IV

What then is the world that we are forbidden to love? It is not a tangible and visible thing at all. To love the world, as another has pointed out, is to be brought into bondage to that something in the world that keeps the world from being Christ-like. What is it that keeps this every-day life that we are living in the here and now from being heavenly? It is this: there are so many of us that are selfish. There are so many of us that are putting forth our utmost endeavours to please ourselves. Self-pleasing is the spirit that dominates the world, and to love the world is to be brought under dominion of this spirit of self-pleasing. So that the text might read: "Demas forsook me, having desired to do as he pleased."

Now this desire to please ourselves does not always lead in the same direction. But it always leads away from God. The Prodigal Son was brought under the dominion of this spirit, and was thus led away into the Far Country. His elder brother remained very decently at home, but he was under the dominion of the same spirit, the spirit of selfishness. One man may live for his own ends and go to the gutter. His neighbour may live under the dominion of exactly the same motives and go to Congress. The significant matter is not the differing goals, but the common motive that is back of the arrival at both goals.

As Demas worked at Paul's side over in the great city

of Rome, he began to feel this love of the world tugging at his heart. His friend, Paul, was always consulting the higher Will. He was always subjecting himself to the doing of Christ's will instead of his own. Demas began to grow tired of it. There were people all about him in Rome who were going their own way and seemingly making a great success of it. He could not shut his eyes to this fact. He could not keep from asking himself: "Why cannot I taste life as they are tasting it and enjoy life as they seem to be enjoying it?"

It is night and these two saints are walking down the streets of Rome on their way to church. About them are the splendours of a city that has grown drunk upon the vintage of the wide world. The atmosphere is perfumed with pleasure and is vocal with the joyous laughter of the gay. Soldiers are passing laden with the spoils of war. Beauty is passing, offering her charms for the taking. And Paul walks breast forward and seems never to see the gay sights about him. But Demas sees. And as he sees he begins to wonder if he had not better "take the cash and let the credit go."

But the lights are growing dimmer and the streets are narrower. At last they come to a place as weird and dreary and repulsive as a tomb. It is a tomb—one of the catacombs. And a few of the saints with faces strangely alight are there for service. Demas sits down among them, but there is not the joy in this meeting with God's people that he once knew. In spite of himself he is out on the brilliantly lighted streets again. Suddenly his mind is recalled from the gay scenes without to what Paul is saying: "The things that are seen are temporal, but the things that are not seen are eternal." "This great city of Rome that seems so abiding is only a passing show. A few more years and a bit of wreckage and a stain of blood and a handful of bones will be all that will be left to tell that a caravan called Rome passed this way and camped for a night and then went into utter silence forever." And Demas said: "I wonder. Paul may be right, but I doubt it."

A few days later Demas' place is empty. He has fallen in love with the world. His heart has gone to the world and he has followed his heart. Desiring to please himself, he has left Paul and Paul's Christ and has journeyed to Thessalonica. He wants a life that is more colourful, more gay, less dull and drab and leaden. He is in love with the world. Therefore, he is going to take the way that he believes will most surely minister to his desire to laugh and revel and to enjoy. Paul may hold on to his life for Christ, but he is going to please himself for a while. And so he goes the way of the world.

You remember that rather strange condition that the father of Portia decided upon for the marriage of his daughter. Her picture was to be put in one of three caskets, and the suitor who chose the casket in which the likeness was found was to win her hand. One casket was of gold, the other of silver, the other of lead. The first had upon it this motto: "Who chooses me shall get what many men desire." The second, the silver, had this motto: "Who chooses me shall get as much as he deserves." The third, made of base lead, had this forbidding inscription: "Who chooses me must give and hazard all he hath."

You can readily see the difference in these inscriptions. The first two are practically alike: "Who chooses me shall get what many men desire." "Who chooses me shall get as much as he deserves." They both appeal to the man whose supreme passion is getting. But the

third says: "Who chooses me must give and hazard all
he hath." That appeals to one whose passion is giving.
And the picture was in the leaden casket. It was the
only way that this wise old father had of reaching a
hand from the grave and holding his daughter back
from the deep damnation of marrying a "getter."

V

Demas chose the golden casket. Demas became a
"getter." As such he left Paul and went to Thessalonica. What became of him after this we do not know.
For the sake of argument, however, we are going to as-
sume that loving the world, he won it. I imagine the
most palatial house in Thessalonica was the house in
which Demas lived. The finest carpets were the carpets
that were upon his floors, and the finest tapestry was
that that adorned his walls. And there were no feasts
in all the city like the feasts that were given by Demas,
the one-time friend and fellow-worker of St. Paul.

One night I attended one of these marvellous feasts,
and those that Demas had gathered about him were the
gayest of the gay. They belonged to the highest social
set of the city. And Demas entertained as one to the
manor born. But when the guests were all gone and
I went to congratulate him upon the great success of
his entertainment, I found him with care lines deep
in his face, and with an attitude so eloquent of heartache that I longed to cheer him up a bit. So I hastened to say, "Demas, I congratulate you upon your
vast wealth. But I wish you might meet a friend of
mine. I am sorry to say that he is in prison over in
Rome. His name is Paul. He is a great joy bringer."

And the soul of Demas stood up in his eyes and he

said: "Do you know Paul? I used to know him. The one oasis in this desert life of mine is the time I spent in his fellowship. The one bit of spring in this dreary and bleak winter was the time that I spent by his side. God forgive me for ever having left him. A thousand times while I have been money-grubbing here in Thessalonica I would have given every dirty dollar to have been at his side again as I was before the day of my shameful desertion."

And I turn away from this chilling atmosphere to look into a prison cell where Paul is being held. He is writing a letter. And as he writes a chilling breeze comes in through the prison window and fans the thin hair about his temples and I see him shiver. But he writes on. Again the breeze comes, but stronger and colder. And he feels behind him as if searching for a wrap, and then he smiles and says to himself: "Oh, my cloak. I remember now I left it at Troas with Carpus." And he writes: "Dear Timothy: 'The cloak that I left at Troas with Carpus, when thou comest, bring with thee. And do thy best to come before winter.'"

Poor aged Paul. I find it in my heart to pity him. But he pauses in his writing to look out a window. It is the window that looks into the past. It is a past of which he is not ashamed. There is many a sacrifice in it, many a conflict, many a persecution, many a sleepless night, many a tear. But the old hero looks upon it all with a smile, and then takes up his pen and writes: "I have fought the good fight; I have finished my course; I have kept the faith."

Here he pauses again and looks out through another window. It is the window that looks into the future. The scene that meets his gaze makes his face brighter still. It is coronation day on the "other side," and among those who are being crowned he sees himself. And again he writes: "Henceforth there is laid up for me a crown of righteousness, which the Lord, the righteous judge, shall give me on that day. And not to me only, but unto all them also that love his appearing." And as for me, I would like to take my stand anew this morning beside Paul, and, above all else, beside Paul's Christ.

IV

WHITE FEATHERS—MARK

II Timothy 4 : 11

"Take Mark and bring him with thee: for he
is profitable unto me for the ministry."

I

Did you notice the name of the man for whom Paul
is calling? Paul, you know, is in the midst of trying
circumstances. He is in prison. He is surrounded by
dangers. Death is rattling the latch of his door. He
needs men about him who are to be trusted. Fair
weather friends are of no avail now. Parlour soldiers
count for less than nothing. He must have as his
helpers men of steady courage, men of hardy heroism,
men who stand ready to pay the last measure of devotion.

And when he looks about over his wide circle of
acquaintances for a man of this type, for whom does
he write? On whom does he call? Listen! "Take
Mark and bring him with thee: for he is profitable
unto me for the ministry." You read the sentence with
a gasp of amazement. Can it be that John Mark is
profitable? Can it be that the worthless has become
worthful? Has this useless young fellow become useful? Has this human liability changed into an asset?
For the last we heard of John Mark he was far

from being the type of man that we should call upon in a situation that demanded men of heroic mould.

About a dozen years ago 'when Paul and Barnabas were on the point of setting out on a second missionary journey, this man Mark offered his services, but Paul would not accept. He did not say then, "Mark is profitable unto me for the ministry." He said the opposite. Here is what we read: "Paul thought it not good to take him." Paul thought John Mark by his presence would add nothing at all. He did not think his joining the expedition would be of the least value. If you had asked him his opinion of this young man, Mark, he would have been obliged to tell you in all sincerity that he looked upon him as absolutely useless.

Not only did he regard him as useless, but as worse than useless. In a trying situation he would only be in the way. Instead of being an asset he would be a liability. Instead of being a help, he would be a hindrance. Paul loved Barnabas for many reasons. He loved him, in the first place, because Barnabas was genuinely lovable. Then Barnabas had befriended Paul at a time when friendship counted. When Paul went to Jerusalem the first time after his conversion, everybody suspected him. That is, everybody with one exception, and that one exception was Barnabas. Barnabas believed in him and stood by him.

Later when Barnabas went down to Antioch and saw how God was working in that great city, he sought some capable man as an assistant. The one to whom he turned was Paul. He introduced Paul to this vigorous church at Antioch. Then he and Paul had gone forth on their first missionary journey together. They had been brothers in a common enterprise. They had

been the seers of a common vision, the dreamers of
a common dream. They had preached together and
prayed together and suffered together. They had been
brought together in the bonds of a very intimate and
tender fellowship.

There is no doubt that Paul loved Barnabas greatly.
There is no doubt that this "son of consolation" was a
tremendous help to Paul. But, as dearly as Paul loved
Barnabas, and as helpful as he found him, he declared
that he would rather go on his missionary journey alone
than to go with Barnabas and John Mark. That is,
he considered that John Mark would be a greater hindrance than Barnabas would be a help. He greatly
desired the inspiring and bracing fellowship of Barnabas, but he had rather surrender that than be hampered
and held back by that soft millstone, John Mark.

So it is very evident that at this time Paul had no
admiration for Mark. He thought any missionary enterprise would be weakened rather than strengthened
by his presence. He was firmly convinced that to have
such a man as his assistant would mean a weight rather
than wings. Yet some ten or twelve years later we
find him speaking again of this man, and his tone
is utterly changed. Instead of saying that Mark is
useless, instead of declaring that he is not only useless but a positive hindrance, he writes about him this
surprising and thrilling sentence: "Take Mark and
bring him with thee: for he is profitable unto me for
the ministry."

II

How did Paul come to change his opinion of Mark?
How has he come to believe in the heroism of this

man whom he at one time considered so unheroic? How
has he come to believe in the usefulness of this man
whom yesterday he regarded as altogether worthless?
Answer: Paul had not changed. Mark had changed.
Mark had been remade. This bit of human waste had
become wealth.

It would be well to ask how Paul came to think so
meanly of Mark in the beginning. Certainly he did
not distrust him without reason. Paul had had experience with Mark. He knew him well. When Paul
and Barnabas had set out on their first missionary enterprise, this young man was selected as their assistant.
He had been greatly trusted; he had been signally honoured by his Lord and by his Church.

This missionary campaign launched by Barnabas and
Paul and Mark was the first that was enterprised by
the Christian Church. Many thousands of heroic souls
have gone forth on a like mission since then. They
have crossed all seas. They have penetrated all for-
ests. They have preached in all nations. They have
laid their ashes on all shores. But at the vanguard of
this noble army of heroes walked these three men,
Barnabas and Paul and John Mark. Certainly John
Mark had been greatly trusted; certainly he had been
highly honoured.

What response did he make to this great confidence?
He proved utterly unworthy. He went over to the
Island of Cyprus with his two friends. From there
he sailed with them to the Continent and landed at
Perga. By this time the romance of the adventure
had altogether vanished. By this time he saw that the
delightful lark upon which he fancied himself enter-
ing when he left Antioch was a stern and exacting campaign. No sooner had he reached the city of Perga

than he made haste to turn his back on his friends and
on their discomforts and their hardships and make his
way to the restful home of his mother in Jerusalem.

So, you see, Mark was a quitter. God and His Church
had honoured him with a task, but he threw it down.
They had trusted him with a position of responsibility
and he had turned his back upon it. He did very well
when nothing was expected of him except to parade,
but when the real fight came he threw down his weapons
and fled. He was like that contemptible character in
Shakespeare who said, "But for these vile guns, I
would have been a soldier."

III

Why did Mark quit?

He did not do so because his two friends wanted him
to quit. Paul and Barnabas did not drive him away
from their presence. They did not wrong him and
wound him and make his work an impossibility. He
could not say when he got home, "I quit because of the
unbrotherly treatment of those with whom I was sent
to serve." Nor did he quit because he concluded that
his presence was no longer needed. Mark knew the
trying situation in which his two friends were labouring. He knew the odds against them as two lone men
they faced the vast heathen millions. He knew that
while the harvest indeed was plenteous, the labourers
were pathetically few. He knew that he was needed.
He knew that he could render a real service if he would
only stand by. But in spite of this fact he left. But
he did not leave because he was convinced he was not
needed.

Why did he leave? We are not told explicitly. Of

this we are sure, however, that there was no justifiable excuse for his leaving. Had he had a good reason Paul would not have censured him as he did. And yet Paul did censure him most severely. Certain it is that he could give no reason for his conduct that would pass muster. In no way could he justify his having played the rôle of a quitter. And in this respect he is like those among ourselves who have quit. No man can justify himself for withdrawing from the fight and giving over the battle. No man can justify deliberate idleness. "To him that knoweth to do good and doeth it not, to him it is sin."

As we read between the lines, we are convinced of this: that Mark quit because he was afraid of the hardship, of the self-denial, of the dangers that confronted him. He had been raised in a home of wealth. Doubtless he had been considerably spoiled. He had possibly had too much petting. He was a bit soft. When he found that being a missionary meant downright hardship, that it meant privations, hard work and facing danger, he decided that the enterprise was too costly. He made up his mind that he would not pay the price. So he threw down his task and set out for home.

Thus he became John Mark, the Quitter. But he is not the only quitter. Their name is legion to this hour. Some of them are in the Church. When you became a member of the Church years ago you were full of enthusiasm. You were ready for any good work. For a while you made a business of your religion. You considered the services of the Church not as the responsibility of the pastor alone, but as a responsibility of yourself also. But little by little the fires died upon the altar of your soul. To-day, though you are still in the Church, you do not count. If everybody treated the prayer meeting as you treat it, there would not be another held to the end of time. If everybody treated the night service as you treat it, there would not be another church lighted for service until this old world became a cinder. Many of the quitters among us are those who have moved away from their old home churches into the city and have left their membership behind. Every city abounds in these. Our own denomination loses thousands of members in this fashion every year. I am told that in a single block in one of our large cities a religious census revealed the fact that there were thirteen hundred men and women who had once been actively engaged in various Protestant Churches, every single one of whom had quit.

Why had these quit ? If I were able to talk with each of them individually, I should doubtless hear many excuses. But I dare to say the most of them, were they to give the real reason, would give that that lay back of the desertion of John Mark. They simply have not devotion enough to the Cause of Christ and His Kingdom to be willing to pay the price. They are not willing to bear the burden and to face their responsibilities. They are unwilling to meet that test of discipleship laid down by the Master Himself: "If any man will come after me, let him deny himself and take up his cross daily and follow me." The Bishop of London was entirely correct when he said some years ago that our modern Christianity is terribly lacking in the element of heroism. "Were it not for the fact," says he, "that the cross of Jesus

Christ can be made into a lovely ornament to wear about our necks instead of an ugly instrument of torture upon which we are to die to self and to the world, we would have thrown it away long ago." Mark was afraid of the Cross. And that fear has gripped many of us in pulpit and in pew to this day.

IV

But what says Paul of this man who deserted his post? What is it he is writing about this quitter? Listen! "Take Mark and bring him with thee: for he is profitable unto me for the ministry." Then Mark has come back. The coward of yesterday has become the hero of to-day. That is amazing! That is wonderful! That is a story full of thrilling hope for ourselves. If God could make a weak man into a tower of strength yesterday, if He could make a coward into a hero yesterday, then He can do the same for us to-day.

How do we account for the recovery of Mark?

1. I think it probable that the most effective agency that God used in the re-making of John Mark was the Apostle Paul. Barnabas was a tremendously helpful man, always generous, always determined to think the best. But it is altogether possible that his generosity was hurtful to Mark rather than helpful. It rather humoured his cowardice than rebuked it. Mark had a great tendency to be soft and indolent and weak. He needed somebody to cut him to the quick. He needed a good sharp rebuke. He did not need a sedative to put him more soundly to sleep. He needed to be shaken into wakefulness.

This, by God's help, Paul did for him. When Paul

refused to endanger his enterprise by taking such a weakling with him, when Paul told him frankly and lovingly what he thought of him, Mark began to come to himself. He began to see himself as he really was, to realise how hideously he had sinned. And until he was brought to that realisation, there was no hope for him. Mark needed this seeming harshness on the part of Paul. There are times when the greatest cruelty we can do our friends is to be too gentle and too kind to tell them the truth. Many a man has been saved by having some brave Paul or some brave Nathan to look him squarely in the eye and tell him exactly what is wrong.

2. I am persuaded that Peter had no small part in Mark's recovery. When Mark had been made to realise his sin, and when his head was bowed with shame and his heart was broken, then it was Peter that could speak to him better than any one else. For Peter had had an awful fall himself. Peter had himself been a quitter. He had known what it was to make a terrible and disgraceful failure.

You can almost see this kind old preacher with his hand on the bowed head of John Mark while he is talking to him. "Yes, my son, I know. One time I boasted to my Lord that I was ready to go with Him to prison and to death. And a few hours later a little servant girl asked me if I was a disciple of His. Of course I had been perfectly confident of what my answer would be to that question. I had been absolutely sure a little while before of what I would say under the circumstances. I was going to say: 'Certainly I am His disciple. It is the one thing of which I am most proud. I am prouder of it than I am of my own life. I am so proud of it that I would

gladly die for Him.' But I said nothing of the kind.
My heart failed within me. Panic seized me and I
lied and said that I had never known Him. But, you
know, my boy, even then, Christ did not throw me
away; He did not cast me off. He passed by and
looked at me and I saw in that tender look the yearning of a broken heart. And my knees went weak
and my throat choked with sobs, and my eyes filled
with tears, and I went out and wept bitterly. And,
you know, He forgave me. And when He was risen
from the dead, this is what He said: 'Go tell my disciples and Peter.' He took me back and let me go on
in His work, and that is what He will do for you."

And Mark heard and believed and started again.
And the mighty Christ took hold of him, and the man
who yesterday was useless and worse than useless became profitable. He was profitable to Peter. He was
profitable to Paul. And through the long centuries he
has been profitable to an innumerable company. Only
yesterday you were reading a little book. It was the
first Gospel ever written. And as you turned the pages
you had a wonderfully clear glimpse of Christ, and
you thanked God for the book, and then you thanked
God for the author of the book. And when you thanked
God for the author, you were thanking Him for John
Mark. Yes, this useless man, Mark, has become a
blessing and will continue to be a blessing to the end
of the ages.

v

And the fact, my brethren, that Mark came back
is most heartening to me. It gives me hope for myself. It gives me hope for you. For we have all failed

somewhat; we have all been in some measure quitters.
We have all come short of the glory of God. We must
realise that this is true. In an Old Book I read this
sentence, "He shall not fail." And when I read it I
knew the writer was not talking about either you or
myself, for we have both failed. We have not done
our best. We have not realised our largest possibilities.
In some measure we are failures.

What hope is there for us failures? This big hope.
We may start again. The difference between the finally
defeated and the finally successful is not so much in
the fact that one sinned and the other did not. It
is in the fact that one had the courage to begin again
while the other let one great failure overcome him. Just
remember this: that no failure need be final.

> "Each day is a new beginning.
> Each morn is the world made new,
> Oh, ye who are weary of sinning,
> Here's a hope and a chance for you."

If you will dare start again this morning, Jesus Christ
will take you back and remake you by His power.

There is a story of three lieutenants who near the
outbreak of the World War belonged to a British regiment. As the war clouds began to gather one of these
young officers was seized with the sickening fear that
when the test of battle came he would prove a coward
and would be utterly unable to face fire. So firmly
was he gripped by this conviction that he succeeded
through the influence of his father, who was a man high
in political life, in getting himself released from the
army.

Having retired from the service, he went to Ireland
where he was engaged to be married to a charming and

spirited girl. One day as they were standing talking
the postman entered and handed him a little neatly-
wrapped package. Upon opening it there floated out
two tiny white feathers. The girl laughed a ringing
laugh and asked for an explanation. And the ex-lieu-
tenant was honest enough to meet the issue squarely.
He told her that they were sent by his two friends in
the army in token of his cowardice. At once the laughter vanished from the lips of the girl. Instead, two
hectic spots burned upon her cheek. And breaking off
a little white spray from the plume of her hat, she
handed it to him and turned and walked away without a
word. The young fellow stood alone under the weight
of his shame. Then he squared his jaw, picked up the
three white feathers, put them back in the box, wrapped
the package, slipped it into his pocket, and hurried
back to England where he joined the army under an
assumed name.

A few weeks later he found himself, by the chances
of war, a part of his old regiment. Then one night
there was an excursion into "No Man's Land," and
one of his lieutenant friends did not come back. He
asked for the privilege of going after him. The officer
in charge replied that it would be suicide, but gave him
permission to go. He went and came. And when he
laid the young officer down on the floor of the trench,
the dying man whispered, "Tom, I knew you would
come back. I knew you were not a coward." And
Tom fumbled in his bosom and brought out a box and
gave the dying soldier one white feather, and he clutched
it in his chilling hand as he "went West."

Other days passed and there was a charge over the
top, and then a stinging pain in head and shoulder.
And when the young fellow came to himself he was in

a shell hole half on and half under a wounded comrade. His companion was crying piteously for water. He shook his canteen and found it had only enough for one. So he put it to the lips of his companion and let him drain the last drop. Then he looked at him closely and recognised his other lieutenant friend. And as consciousness slipped away, he put into his hands a white feather that when they were found was stained by their common blood.

Then with his painful wounds he was invalided home. One day when he came out from being decorated with the Victoria Cross, among those who greeted him was a beautiful Irish girl who wore the garb of a Red Cross nurse. And as he passed her he handed her a little box stained with the mud and the blood of the trenches. When she reached the secrecy of her room that night and opened it, she found in it one white feather, and she knew that the quitter had come back and the coward had become a hero. Thus it was with Mark. And thus it may be with all the Marks here present. However great a failure you have been, you may yet have written of you this sentence: "He is profitable for the ministry."

V

THE BELOVED PHYSICIAN—LUKE

II Timothy 4:11

"Only Luke is with me."

The text is a strange mingling of songs and sobs. It laughs out loud with irrepressible gladness. It also sighs with a grief that is soaked in tears. There is sunshine in it, bright as the splendours of cloudless noon. There is also darkness in it akin to that of a night without stars. Here is a bit of spring-time, a-riot with colour and fragrance and tuneful with the song of birds. Here also is bleak winter, colourless and cold, with the bitter winds wailing through the skeleton boughs of the trees.

"Only Luke is with me." Whence the tearfulness of this sentence? Why is it grief-filled as the heart of a mother who has lost her first-born? For this reason it tells of absent ones whom the Apostle misses and for whose presence he deeply longs. Some of these are away on errands of service; they are away on missions upon which he has sent them. He misses them, and yet there is joy in their very absence. They are at the post of duty. But there is one whom he misses who is not at the post of duty. Yesterday he was here. To-day he is away. And the Apostle cannot keep back his tears as he writes, "Demas hath forsaken me, having loved this present world." "Only Luke is with me."

But while the old hero weeps as he writes this sentence, his tears flow over a face that is still bright with an inner joy. For even though Demas has gone, even if the love of the world has gripped him, even if in this Vanity Fair called Rome, he has forgotten his high quest and has deserted his old friend, there is still one who is faithful and true. If Demas has proved unreliable, if he has turned his back upon friend and duty and God, there is one who still stands by with unshaken loyalty. There is one who remains steadfast. There is one upon whose fidelity he can count with absolute confidence. The crowd may pass him by in utter forgetfulness, his friends may be ashamed of his chain, but there is one who will never be ashamed. And so, with inner laughter, he writes, "Luke is with me."

II

Who is Luke?

Who is this man upon whom Paul counts with such absolute assurance? Is he one who is bound to the Apostle by close ties of flesh and blood? No, Luke and Paul are no kin. Are they brought together by the bonds of a common nationality? No, Paul is a Jew and Luke is a Gentile. A few years ago they were separated by the very widest of chasms. And yet we find them here bound together by the closest bonds of friendship and of brotherhood. They are brothers because they are worshippers of a common Lord. They have experienced the redeeming love of a common Saviour. They who yesterday were afar off both from each other and from God have been brought near by the blood of Christ.

When did Luke become a Christian? We do not know. How was he converted? Here again we must answer that we do not know. But of this we can speak with absolute assurance. Luke is converted now. That man watching outside Paul's prison cell has a present experience of the saving grace of Jesus Christ. And, mark you, that is the important matter. A very earnest man said to me not long ago that he would not give the snap of his finger for the Christianity of any man who could not tell the day and the hour in which he was converted. It is good to know when you were converted, but it is not necessary. There is something far more important than that. It is this: to know that you are converted now. You may have a very clear memory of how Jesus Christ came into your life a quarter of a century ago, but that is of no avail unless He has a place in your heart to-day. It is well to be able to sing "At the Cross where I first saw the light." But it is far better to be able to sing "Blessed Assurance, Jesus is Mine."

Some of you good mothers have been married almost half a century. Suppose when you get home to-day your husband should tell you how beautiful you were years ago when he led you a blushing bride across the threshold of his home. Suppose he were to grow enthusiastic about how charming you looked before you had divided the roses upon your cheek with daughters that are now mothers, and before you had given your strength to sons that are now fathers. There would be little thrill in all that unless he should pass on to tell you of his feelings toward you now. You would want to hear him say: "Though 'the last feather of the raven's wing has fallen from your hair,' and though there are more wrinkles on your face than there are graves in the cemetery over which we have wept together, still you are more beautiful and far dearer than you were on that distant day when love's morning had its dawn."

And it is the present tense of your Christian experience that is of supreme value. How you were converted, when you were converted, where you were converted, all these questions are interesting, but they are not essential. The only big question is, "Do you know Jesus now?" Can you look into His face this moment and say, "My Lord and my God"? If you can do that, you need never worry yourself about dates. If you can do that, you need never worry yourself about the findings of the critics. A young fellow from our Southland came home from the war to find a big writeup of himself in the paper, telling how and when he was killed at the battle-front. The article was well written and sounded altogether truthful. But the living soldier did not accept the statement of the paper, even though the article was written by one who was evidently both cultured and honest. We know that Luke was a Christian because we see him living the life.

III

Another fact that we know about him is that he was a physician. No doubt he was a practising physician before he was ever converted to Christianity. When Jesus got hold of him He did not call upon him to throw away his old profession and take up one that was altogether new. He called him to the doing of his old

task under new motives and in the energy of a new
power. It is true that Dr. Luke performed other services that are not peculiar to the medical profession.
But it was as a physician that he performed these services. A physician he was at the time of his conversion
and a physician he remained to the end of the day.

And Luke's case is not peculiar. The call of God to
most of us is not into new fields of service. Of course
for some to yield to God is to be called into the ministry.
For others to yield is to be called into the foreign field.
But for most of us to put ourselves into Christ's hands
is to toil at our same task, to work in the way in which
we have been working, but to do that in the inspiration
of a new power and in the joy of a new fellowship.
Dorcas does not throw away her needle when she becomes a Christian. She simply consecrates it to Christ.
Luke does not throw away his bandages and his healing
medicines. He uses them to the glory of God. The
business man does not quit his business. He conducts
it as a good steward of Jesus Christ.

God does not want all of us to do the same thing.
We cannot all render the same service. But we can
all render some service. Dr. Luke cannot preach like
Paul, neither can Paul heal like Luke. This kind physician has a task all his own. And it would be hard to
find one that is capable of being used more to the glory
of God. The physician who goes to his work as God's
man carries something to his patients that is better
than his skill, however skilful he may be. Blessed
the patient that falls into the hands of a physician
whose powers have been dedicated to his Lord. There
is no end to the service that is rendered by such a
man. He is a fellow worker with the Great Physician.

IV

But Dr. Luke did more than practise medicine. He was a writer of great brilliancy and power. Thus he has brought the whole world into his debt. There are sixty-six books in the Bible. Sixty-four of them were written by Jews. Only two of them were written by a Gentile, and the Gentile that wrote these two was Dr. Luke, the Christian Physician. And these two books are about as choice bits of literature as even the Word of God contains. It is to Luke we are indebted for the thrilling story of the conquest of the early Church. It is he that tells of the coming of the Promise of the Father on the day of Pentecost. It is Luke who tells us of Peter's inspired sermon on that day, and of the conversion of the three thousand. It is Luke who lets us into the intimate fellowship of the great saints of that day—Paul, Peter, Barnabas, and others.

Then we are indebted to Luke for the third Gospel. Renan called this Gospel of Luke the most beautiful book ever written. It tells of course the same story as that told by the other evangelists, and yet there are touches that make it far different. Luke was not writing to the Jews, but to the Gentiles. He was writing especially for ourselves. Naturally he does not place his emphasis always where the other evangelists place theirs. He goes beyond them, as others have pointed out, in giving emphasis to at least two important truths.

1. It is Luke who emphasises the universality of Christ's forgiving love. Matthew makes the wise men ask, "Where is He that is born King of the Jews?"

Matthew has the Jews in his eye as he writes. But when Luke writes the story he gives no prominence to the Jewish claim. "And lo, the Angel of the Lord came upon them, and the glory of the Lord shone round about them; and they were sore afraid. And the Angel said unto them, Fear not: for, behold, I bring you good tidings of great joy, which shall be to all people. For unto you is born this day in the city of David a Saviour, which is Christ the Lord." Then Luke proceeds to tell us story after story in which he emphasises the fact that his good tidings are really meant for all the people.

Down in the rich city of Jericho there was a man named Zaccheus. This man was a publican. He had sold himself to a foreign power. He wore the livery of Rome, and, therefore, he was more despised than if he had worn the garb of a slave. This man was rich, but he was an outcast. He was rich, but he was hated and shunned, and every door to decency was shut in his face. But one day Jesus Christ came that way and invited Himself to be a guest in the home of this despised grafter. And Jesus Christ said to him: "To-day is salvation come to thy house." Luke is the only one that tells us this story.

Then one night there is a feast in the house of a certain Pharisee. Jesus is a guest. During the meal there is a disturbance. A berouged woman of the street steals in from out the dark. She falls down at the feet of Jesus and washes them with her tears. Then she undoes the cascade of her hair and wipes those feet with the hairs of her head. And Simon, the Pharisee, shudders with horror because the Master allows Himself to be touched by this soiled rag of womanhood. But Jesus declares that her sins that are many are forgiven because she loves much. We owe that precious bit to Luke.

But the finest story ever written has not yet been mentioned. It begins like this: "A certain man had two sons, and the younger of them said to his father, Give me the portion of goods that falleth to me. And he divided unto them his living. And not many days after the younger son gathered all together and took his journey into a far country, and there wasted his substance in riotous living." It is needless to tell the whole story. It is about the most familiar in the literature of the world. And the reason it is so familiar is because, above all other stories, it reveals the compassionate and tender heart of our Heavenly Father. It tells us how eternally eager He is to give heaven's best even to those who have wasted their substance in riotous living. Luke makes most plain to us the universality of the forgiving love of God.

2. It is Luke also who emphasises the perils of prosperity. Come all you who would be rich and read and re-read the Gospel of Luke. Do you remember that story that Jesus told of the rich farmer? Do you recall the man who was so pressed by the work of barn building that he had no time for soul building? Do you recall him who was so busy piling up treasure for the few days in which he might live that he utterly forgot to make any provision for the eternity in which he must live? Do you recall that shrewd man who one day tumbled into his abundant crops and got drowned just as you have seen a bee get drowned in its own honey? Did you ever sit down and let the Rich Fool tell you what a perilous something is prosperity? It is Luke who has preserved for us this startling story.

It is Luke also who tells us of another very prosperous man called Dives. No charge is made against this man. He is simply shown to us for a typical day in his life. He is dressing well and trying to get rid of some of his money by giving banquets. There is a beggar at his gate, but he does not see him. He is too busy trying to amuse himself. Therefore, he neither helps this beggar nor does he drive him away. He simply lets him alone. Then one day death comes for this rich man, and he leaves his palace dreaming of the bosom of Abraham only to hang his daintily sandalled foot in the rags of the old beggar at his gate and fall flat into hell. Truly Luke forces us to see how right was the Master when He said, "How hardly shall they that have riches enter into the Kingdom of God."

v

What kind of a man was Luke?

1. We would like much to know. But Luke was not good at having his picture made. He took absolutely no pains to leave us a life-size picture of himself. In fact he kept his own face hidden as much as possible. But he revealed this much in spite of himself: that he was a scholar. Luke was one of the best trained men of his time. He was a man of wide reading and accurate information. He was capable of mental fellowship with St. Paul, and St. Paul was one of the intellectual giants of all time. It is true that Luke does not tell us what university he attended, nor what degrees he had. He is too modest for that. But no thoughtful man can read his books without realising that he is reading from a painstaking and well-trained scholar.

2. Another fact that Luke cannot conceal about himself is his beautiful modesty. He lets us into the secret not by what he says, but by what he fails to say. When he wrote his Gospel, for instance, it was necessary for him to interview many notable people. The Virgin Mother was doubtless among these. But he does not tell us so. In fact he never mentions his own name in all the story. And when he wrote The Acts, though he himself was a part of some of the stirring stories that he tells, yet here again his name is never mentioned. There is no use to ask Luke's left hand what his right hand is doing. You will not get the least information. He sees to it that such matters are kept secret. How beautifully Christ-like he is in his modesty! He does the work, but he does not see fit to tell us who did it. He paints the picture, but he does not put his own name in the corner when the job is finished. He presents us with two of the most beautiful and helpful books ever written. But when we look over on the flyleaf we see that he forgot to autograph them. When we turn the pages, though we look carefully, we fail to find any calling card. A modest and scholarly man was Luke.

3. Luke was lovable. Paul calls him the Beloved Physician. And is it not a great privilege to be loved? Why is it that we love some folks? Answer: Some folks are so lovable. There are some people that we cannot resist. We may hear things about them that we do not like. We may come to them with pre-conceived notions and with unfair prejudices, but their presence strikes the death blow to all these enemies of love. Our hearts capitulate and we yield to them in spite of ourselves. Luke was like that. He took the heart of Paul captive, and the heart of many another.

What ammunition did he use? Can you not guess? He used love. There is no conqueror of hearts like that. It is the weapon that God Himself uses for the conquest of you and me. "We love because He first loved us." If you want to be lovable—and that is a prize to be coveted—if you want to be as attractive as a garden caressed by the springtime, if you want to be as sweet and winsome as the music of the mocking bird, then let love into your life. Folks can resist logic; they can resist the best arguments, but they melt like snow at the sun's kiss under the mighty influence of love.

4. Luke was steadfast. He was modest and loving and lovable, but that did not keep him from having the heart of a lion. The touch of his hand was as soft as the touch of a mother, but he was not soft in his moral fibre. He was a man of the hardiest courage. It is a tremendous help in fighting a hard fight to have the companionship of comrades. It is exceedingly encouraging when we are facing danger to know that brave hearts are standing by our side. Luke needed this encouragement, but it was not absolutely essential. "Dr. Luke, Paul has lost his popularity. The crowds have turned from him." "Then," said Luke, "I will do without the crowds. By the grace of God I am able to stand alone."

And Paul, with an appreciation that sets his burdened heart to singing, takes his pen and writes, "Only Luke is with me." What a fine virtue is that of steadfastness. How God needs men and women in the Church that can be relied upon. Every church has a few of this kind. The pastor soon learns them. When the prayer meeting comes, they are there. When the revival comes, they are there. When the day is ugly and stormy and few find their way to God's house, they are among them. They are dependable. They are steadfast. They are those to whom God will be able to say by and by: "You have been faithful." When I see Luke watching alone outside the prison cell of Paul, my heart fairly bows the knee within me in honour of him. Thank God for Luke.

"Only Luke is with me." And the man who writes this pathetic sentence is in disgrace and in prison. But Luke does not choose his friends because of their popularity nor because of their success in the eyes of the world. He may be counted on in the days of prosperity. He may be counted on no less in the days of adversity. A great, brave, loyal soul is he. He is modest, lovable, steadfast. Thus Paul could write of him, "Only Luke is with me." And it is my conviction that if Paul were writing a letter to us to-day from "Life's Other Side," he could say this same word, "Luke is with me." Luke was with him in the battle, he stood by him in death, and these friends have found each other about the Round Table of the King. May God give us something of the winsomeness and the steadfastness of Luke, the Beloved Physician.

VI

LUKEWARM—THE LAODICEAN CHURCHMEN

Revelation 3 : 15-16

"I know thy works that thou art neither cold
nor hot: I would that thou wert cold or hot.
So then because thou art lukewarm, and neither
cold nor hot, I will spew thee out of my mouth."

I

This letter sent by our risen Lord through the
Apostle John to the Church at Laodicea is one of the
most arresting utterances that ever fell from His lips.
We cannot read it intelligently without being stirred.
It tends to lay a strong hand upon us and shake us
into wide wakefulness. It startles us, if we hear it
thoughtfully, like fire bells ringing in the dead of
night.

There is an emotion ascribed to our Lord in this
letter that, so far as I know, is not ascribed to Him
anywhere else in the Word of God. There are times
when Christ is represented as being grieved. There are
times when He is represented as being angry. But
here He is represented as being disgusted. He is not
slightly disgusted, but disgusted to the point of utter
nausea. "So then because thou art lukewarm, and
neither cold nor hot, I will spew thee out of my mouth."
Literally, "I am about to vomit you up."

68

II

Who are those with whom are Lord is so thoroughly
displeased? They are not some daring and outbreak-
ing sinners. So far as we are able to find out, Jesus
Christ never showed the slightest disgust for the very
greatest of sinners. There were many beyond the
pale of decency and respectability, but there was not
one beyond His sympathy and His tender compassion. No sin was black enough to fling its victim beyond the reach of His interest and of His forgiving
love.

That was an awful sin that Peter committed on
the night of Christ's arrest. Before the test came he
had solemnly declared that he was ready to go with
his Master both to prison and to death. But he did
not make good his boast. Confronted by a servant girl
who inquires of his loyalty to Jesus Christ, he refuses
to confess that there has ever been any friendship
between them. Worse still, he swears that he has never
met Jesus at all. And this he did, mark you, when
his Master stood alone and was most sorely in need
of a friend. But what response did Jesus make to
this contemptible and cowardly denial? With what
eyes did He look upon Peter after this?

There was no disgust when He looked upon this
disciple whose knees had gone weak and whose heart
had utterly failed in the presence of danger. He did
not scorn Peter. There was sorrow, there was compassion more tender than ever looked out of the eyes
of a mother, but there was no scorn. That is the
reason this look broke Peter's heart. That is the
reason he went out and wept bitterly. That is the
reason Christ was able to send him this glad word

after His resurrection: "Go tell my disciples and Peter."

One day the Pharisees threw an ugly piece of human wreckage at the Master's feet. She was a woman of blasted character. She had walked to that hour through the stench and filth of a moral swamp. She belonged to that class that in all ages has been the victim of man's keenest scorn and disgust. But Christ was not disgusted with her. He looked upon her with a tenderness that gave her hope. He spoke to her with an encouragement that turned her wavering steps toward the heights. He prophesied for her the dawning of a bright to-morrow. "Neither do I condemn thee. Go and sin no more."

The object of Christ's contempt, then, is not some reckless and aggressive sinner. Strange to say, the object of his contempt is a church. It is a group of religious people who have formed an organisation presumably for the purpose of fighting under His banner and spreading His Kingdom. They are people who call themselves Christians. Not only so, but they pride themselves upon being a very superior grade of Christians. And yet for this group Christ has no word of commendation. He has nothing better to say to them than "I am about to spew thee out of my mouth."

III

Why was Christ disgusted with this church at Laodicea? He has nothing to say against their organisation or against their doctrine. His objection is just this: "Thou art lukewarm." The typical member of the church at Laodicea was neither cold nor hot. He was half-hearted; he was limp, flabby. He had no earnest-

ness, no zeal, no glow, no go. He was not aggressive.
He was a straddler, a sitter on the fence, lukewarm.

IV

Why is Christ so antagonistic to lukewarmness?
Why does He hate it more than positive and aggressive sin? For it is evident that He does so hate it.
Here are His words: "I would that thou wert cold
or hot." Of course our Lord wants us to be out and
out for Him. He wants us to be enthusiastic in His
service. But He declares that if we are not going
to be positively hot, then He desires that we be positively cold. If we are not going to be genuinely for
Him, He desires that we be genuinely against Him.
There is nothing that He so loathes, that He so hates,
as lukewarmness.

1. He hates it because he cannot help hating it.
Lukewarmness, half-heartedness, is in itself offensive
both to God and man. How would you like to see
a football game played between two teams neither of
which had enough interest in the game to care to win?
Who cares to play a game with an antagonist that is
limp and half-hearted?

Who wants such an individual for a friend? Who
cares for such an associate in the social circle? Did
you ever shake hands with one that was so limp that
there would not have been any hand-shake unless you
had done it all? Is there any tang in Hamlet's conversation with Polonius when the old gentleman is
ready to agree that the cloud looks like a camel or
a mouse, or anything else that Hamlet may suggest?

Addison may not have deserved the ugly wound that
Pope inflicted upon him, but he will never recover

from it. Pope has made us feel that the object of his satire is not the type of man we would want as our friend.

> ". . . but were there One whose fires
> True genius kindles, and fair Fame inspires;
> Blest with each talent and each art to please,
> And born to write, converse, and live with ease:
> Should such a man, too fond of rule alone,
> Bear, like the Turk, no brother near the throne.
> View him with scornful, yet with jealous eyes,
> And hate for arts that caus'd himself to rise;
> Damn with faint praise, assent with civil leer;
> And without sneering, teach the rest to sneer;
> Willing to wound, and yet afraid to strike,
> Just hint a fault, and hesitate dislike;
> Alike reserv'd to blame, or to commend,
> A tim'rous foe, and a suspicious friend;
>
> .   .   .   .
>
> Who but must laugh, if such a man there be?
> Who would not weep, if Atticus were he?"

2. Not only does Christ hate lukewarmness because it is hateful in itself, but because it robs its victim of all possibility of progress. This is true because lukewarmness is a child of self-satisfaction. That is evident from the letter before us. The members of this church were well satisfied, they were content with themselves. They said: "We are rich and increased in goods, and have need of nothing." They had all the knowledge of God and all the spiritual power and all the usefulness that they cared to have. They were sure that they had arrived.

Now such self-satisfaction means death to earnestness. No enthusiasm is possible for such an individual. Not only does this mean death to earnestness, but it means arrested development. It means death to progress. For if you know as much as you want to know, you will not likely learn any more. If you are as good as you want to be, you will not get any better. If you are as high up the hill as you care to be, you will not climb any higher. If you are winning the world to Christ as rapidly as you want to win it, you will certainly not enlarge your efforts.

Christ never pronounced a blessing on the self-satisfied. He did pronounce one on him who hungers and thirsts after righteousness. He declared that such should be filled. If you are fully content to be what you are, if you have no conscious need, then you make it impossible for Christ to bless you and lead you into a richer spiritual life.

That is what our Lord meant when He told about those two men that went to church one day. One of them was a respectable man and the other was an outcast. One of them was honest and the other was a grafter. Yet on a certain Sabbath morning both of these men went to church. One of them, the decent, respectable man, entered the church as if it were his own. He went well up to the front and prayed after this fashion: "God, I thank thee that I am not as other men, extortioners, unjust, adulterers. I fast twice in the week. I give tithes of all I possess." There was no aspiration after a larger goodness in his prayer. He was well pleased with himself. Therefore, he went home as he came. There was no song in his soul and no light in his face.

But the other man, the publican, came to God's

house goaded on by a great need. He felt that his burden was too heavy for him to bear. He felt his sin as an ugly offence against God, and as a gnawing agony to his own soul. Every man might be ahead of him in goodness, but no man passed him in point of being in need. And so this poor, broken man slipped into God's house. He did not go well up to the front, but stood afar off and smote upon his breast and prayed: "God, be merciful to me a sinner." And what was the result? "He went down to his house justified." The peace that passeth all understanding had come into his heart. This was made possible because he came before God with the burning thirst of a man conscious of his need.

3. Not only does Jesus hate lukewarmness because it is hateful, and because it is a foe to all progress, He hates it because it kills our possibilities of usefulness. The battles for the spread of the Kingdom of Christ are all won by those who are in earnest. Lukewarm water never wrecked an engine, neither did it ever move one. It is the soul on fire that fires other souls. It is the whole-hearted man that moves mountains of difficulty. When impossibilities see an earnest man coming, they take to their heels. When such a man gets on his knees to pray "the Angels open the windows."

> "Somebody said that it couldn't be done,
>   But he with a chuckle replied,
>   That maybe it couldn't, but he would be one
>   Who wouldn't say so till he'd tried.
>   So he buckled right in with a trace of a grin
>   On his face. If he worried, he hid it,
>   He started to sing as he tackled the thing
>   That couldn't be done, and he did it.

"Somebody scoffed: 'Oh, you'll never do that,
At least no one has ever done it.'
But he took off his coat and he took off his hat,
And the first thing he knew he'd begun it,
With the lift of his chin and a bit of a grin,
If any doubt rose he forbid it;
He started to sing as he tackled the thing
That couldn't be done, and he did it.

"There are thousands to tell you it cannot be done,
There are thousands to prophesy failure;
There are thousands to point out, one by one,
The dangers that wait to assail you,
But buckle right in with a bit of a grin,
Just take off your coat and go to it,
Just start in to sing as you tackle the thing
That cannot be done, and you'll do it."

Less than two centuries ago an undersized man came
out of a service in Alger's Gate Street, London. Had
you asked this man about the service, he would have
told you that it was a good service. He might have
gone on to tell you that he felt his heart strangely
warmed, and that he did trust Christ and Christ alone
for salvation; and that an assurance was given unto
him that God had forgiven his sins. And when you
had heard the story, you might have doubted; you might
have passed down the street saying: "He felt his heart
strangely warmed. I wonder if anything will come
of it. Doubtless he will forget all about it by to-
morrow."

But he did not forget. Instead of forgetting, this
man with his hot heart pounding in his bosom mounted
his horse the next day and started on a long journey.
He rode literally through the century. And as he

rode, account for it as you may, the icicles fell from the eves of the houses and the winter-stripped trees put on their verdant foliage, and the birds sang and the flowers bloomed and the human heart stood up in the glad consciousness that God had come. And civilisation moved into a new day because this man got his heart on fire.

v

Is there a cure for lukewarmness? Can the listless life be made earnest? Can our dead enthusiasm be revived? Can the half-hearted man become whole-hearted? He can. Thank God, he can. Christ is as clear in pointing out the remedy as He is in administering His rebuke. Hear Him! "Be zealous, therefore, and repent." "Behold, I stand at the door and knock. If any man will hear my voice and open the door, I will come in to him and sup with him and he with me."

Christ is the cure for lukewarmness. His presence makes half-heartedness an impossibility. "The zeal for God's house burned him up." His passion for man sent Him to the cross. His enthusiastic love for others made Him glad to die. And this earnest Christ and lukewarmness cannot home in the same heart. If Christ comes in, then this disgusting foe of our progress and of our usefulness must go out.

Will you accept this remedy? "Behold, I stand at the door and knock." Notice the tense. It is not "Behold, I have stood at the door and knocked." That would of course be true. Christ has knocked at the door of some of our hearts for years. He knocked through all yesterday. He has been knocking through the hours of this blessed Sabbath. But His knocking is not all in the past, neither is it a great expectation for the future. It is a blessed fact of to-day, of this present moment. "Behold, I am now standing at the door and knocking." If you will open the door and let Jesus in, your lukewarmness will vanish as wintertime vanishes at the kiss of spring.

VII

THE BUSINESS WOMAN—LYDIA

Acts 16 : 14

"And a certain woman named Lydia, a seller
of purple, of the city of Thyatira, which wor-
shipped God, heard us: whose heart the Lord
opened, that she attended unto the things which
were spoken of Paul."

I

Lydia is one of the choicest characters of the New
Testament. She grips us with her winsome womanli-
ness. This is true in spite of the fact that she was a
business woman. She had a home, but her task was
not primarily that of a home-maker. If she was ever
married, she has become a widow when we make her
acquaintance. She toils not in the home, but upon
the big world stage. She is engaged in commerce.
She is a live and an alert woman of business.

Because Lydia was in business, her story sounds
very modern. It smacks of to-day rather than of a
far-off yesterday. She was in a small minority then,
but were she living to-day she would find herself a
part of a vast multitude, for roadways lead directly
from a woman's door to-day into all the vocations into
which man has entered. And the number of women
engaged in business other than home-making is in-
creasing daily.

And we are not disposed to find fault with this

situation. There was a time when about the only honorable vocation open to women was that of wifehood and motherhood. But now, thanks to the power of Christ's Gospel, she has come upon a better day. She has found a larger liberty. She has entered upon a larger independence. Once she almost had to marry in order to have a home. To-day this is not necessary. She is thoroughly capable of earning her own way. Hence she does not have to marry unless she so desires.

Not only was Lydia a business woman, but she had made a thorough-going success in business. The record seems to indicate that Lydia was rich. If she had not made a fortune, at least she had succeeded in wisely managing a fortune that had been left to her by another, and this often requires quite as much wisdom and quite as much sagacity as the making of one. She was therefore a woman of keenness and courage. She had real ability. She was perfectly capable of matching wits with her male rivals. And so her sisters have proven themselves in our day. The modern woman has demonstrated the fact over and over again that she is capable of taking her place in the business world alongside of men.

But while Lydia had entered the business world and had won, while she had either made a fortune or had kept one, her struggle and her success had not spoiled her. She had not become mannish. She had not been coarsened by her battle with the world. She had not been swept from her moorings. Though wealthy and successful, she was still religious. We read in the text that she was a worshipper of God.

The modern business woman has not always kept her faith. The liberty that she enjoys has its dangers.

The woman of to-day is not so well protected as her sister of yesterday. The girl who works is oftentimes subjected to temptations of which our mothers knew little. The atmosphere of the business office is not always wholesome. Many a girl has to do her work in an environment the very courseness of which tends to take the fine edge off her modesty. And we cannot deny that many have yielded to the lure of this vulgar atmosphere. We cannot close our eyes to the fact that there are many girls who not only work largely as men work, but sin as men sin. They have become cheap in thought and vulgar in conduct. Sometimes they have degenerated into cigarette smoking and liquor-sipping creatures who are a disgrace to their sex. I must confess, however, that this is not the case so often with the business girl as it is with the society girl who has no business.

But while some business women have been unable to stand the strain, there are vast multitudes that have been able. There are multitudes who have kept both their modesty and their religion. I was once pastor of a church almost half of whose membership was made up of business women. And never have I seen any church better attended in proportion to its membership. Nor have I seen any church whose finances were so easy. There is no bigger asset that the Church of Jesus Christ has to-day than the business woman.

II

How did Lydia come to be a Christian? For, while she was a religious woman when we first met her, she had no knowledge of Christ. She was a follower of the religion of the Jews.

1. She was faithful to the opportunities she had.
She did not have access to a Christian church. There
was not a single Christian in Philippi. She did not
even have access to a Jewish Synagogue. There was
not one in her city. But there was an insignificant
prayer meeting held every Sabbath Day out on a river
bank some miles from the city. It was doubtless a
rather tame and uninteresting affair. There was prob-
ably not much spiritual life in it. Yet Lydia went.
She had the habit of attending these prayer meetings.
Her opportunities were meagre, but she religiously
embraced such opportunities as were within her reach.

It is evident that this business woman made a business of her religion. That is fine. She was not alert
and alive six days in the week and then dead on the
seventh. She was not all interest and enthusiasm in
the market place and listless in the place of prayer.
She was not clear-eyed in the presence of a chance
to buy and sell purple, and bat-eyed when facing an
opportunity to buy "wine and milk without money
and without price." She brought to her religious duties
the same earnestness, the same clear-eyed intelligence
that she brought to her commercial enterprises. Hence,
though in some measure a child of the light, she was
as wise in her generation as the children of the world.

Since Lydia made a business of her religion, we
find her rising with week-day promptness on this Sabbath morning to take her way out to the place of
prayer. She did not know that anything marvellous
was going to happen that day. She did not know that
an event was going to take place that morning that
would make her name remembered when the Empire
of the Cæsars had vanished for centuries. She did not
know that anything would take place out of the ordi-

nary. But, because she thought it was her duty, and because she needed heart help, she went to this prayer meeting that was held by the riverside under the open sky. She was living up to the best she knew. She was using all the light that God had granted her. This made it possible for Him to lead her into the fulness of the light.

The first step, therefore, in Lydia's finding of Christ was her fidelity to the light she already had. The next step came through the ministry of a certain preacher named Paul. God ever works through human instrumentality. He sends His message through human lips. He walks upon his errands of mercy upon human feet. He reaches forth to lift through human hands. For this high task He uses men of every type. He uses educated and uneducated; He uses cultured and uncultured. He uses old and young. He uses the magnetic and the attractive. He uses those who are wanting magnetism. But at least this quality they must have. They must be men ready and willing to obey.

Paul was such a man. When he set out on his missionary journey he had no thought of attending this prayer meeting and speaking to Lydia. He tried to go into Asia, but God shut the door in his face. Then he turned to Bithynia. Again God shut the door in his face. Then there came the call of the man of Macedonia, and immediately, Luke tells us, Paul responded. He set out accompanied by Luke and Timothy and Silas. This army he led from Asia into Europe to claim that important continent for Christ. And no more important army ever crossed any sea or marched into any field.

Why did Paul go to Philippi? Answer: He went

there to help. A man of Macedonia was calling for
help. He did not find that man in the city. Therefore, he set out to the prayer meeting to find him.
Why did Lydia attend this prayer meeting? She was
seeking help. Why was Paul going to attend it? He
was seeking to give help. He was not in search of
fame, though he became famous. He was not in search
of wealth. His one big task was helping. It is for
this reason that he came to the prayer meeting by the
riverside.

Had Paul seen only with the eyes of flesh, he must
have been terribly disappointed in the congregation
that was waiting for him in this prayer meeting. It
was not a large audience. It was a mere handful.
And we love crowds. Every preacher loves a crowd.
There is that in a small audience that tends to depress
us and take the heart out of us. There is that in a
large audience that inspires and creates enthusiasm
and generates hope. But here was only a pitiful little handful, possibly not more than half a dozen.

Not only was this audience depressing in that it was
so small, it was also depressing in that it was made up
entirely of women. There was not a man present.
All the men had gone to the gladiatorial contest, or
to business, or somewhere else. They had not the
slightest interest in this memorable service. That,
however, does not argue the worthlessness of the service.
It rather argues the stupidity and blindness and wick-
edness of the men. The fact that there are far more
men in the penitentiary than women does not prove
that the penitentiary is an altogether desirable place.
No more does the absence of men from this service prove
its worthlessness.

What did Paul do in the presence of this insignificant audience? He might have said: "I am too busy establishing churches and conquering the world to waste my energy here. I will go where I can appeal to the multitudes." But Paul was wise enough to be faithful to the seemingly small opportunity. He was not seeking a place to deliver an oration. He was not seeking for an opportunity to win applause. He was seeking for an opportunity to help. Therefore, he sat down among these women and talked. He did the simple thing that the least gifted and the most timid of us can do. He spoke face to face and heart to heart about the things that were fundamental in his own life.

And as he spoke there was one auditor, one clear-eyed, intelligent woman who listened with peculiar interest. Her rapt attention drew the very best from Paul. He spoke out of the depths of his great heart, and as he spoke a wonderful event took place. It was the greatest event that ever took place in Macedonia. Alexander the Great had marched across its fields, but he had accomplished nothing that is to be compared with what took place in this service. A battle was fought near this spot that decided the history of the civilised world, but even this is insignificant in comparison with the event that took place when Paul spoke to Lydia. For the Lord opened Lydia's heart and she believed. And that was the beginning of Christianity in Europe.

III

Now look at the outcome of this conversion.

1. Lydia brought to Christ all her enthusiasm, all her earnestness, all her fine intelligence and tact. She

was as zealous for Him as she had ever been for herself. Therefore we are not surprised that she won her household to the Lord. She won her children, if she had any. She won her slaves. She won her employés. She at once began to preach the Gospel in her own home and to those associated with her in business, and she won every one of them to her Master.

2. She changed her house into a church. There was no church building in Philippi. The saints were at that time too few in number and too poor to build one. Therefore, this consecrated woman opened her house as a place of worship. It was evidently a roomy place. Lydia might have used it for low forms of social entertainment. With this big house at her disposal she might have shone in the society of that day. But she preferred to dedicate her home with her other possessions to the service of Christ.

3. She also opened her home to give hospitality to Paul and his friends. No man was ever more independent than Paul. He was the farthest possible from being a sponge. He made it a matter of conscience to pay his own way. But Lydia would not let him off. She was bent on being of service. She was determined to give. She had a passion for helping. Therefore, she earnestly urged those saints to make her home their own. Luke says, "She compelled us." Thus Paul and his friends found a home in her house. And thus they were made the freer for the doing of the work to which God had called them.

4. This church that held its services in Lydia's house became one of the most helpful churches that Paul ever founded. We feel safe in saying that no other church was more possessed of the missionary spirit. This church shared in a peculiar way Paul's passion

for world conquest. Nor was there any other church so bent on serving the Apostle himself. It was this church that "sent once and again" unto Paul's necessity while he was at Thessalonica. It was this church that remembered him so helpfully while he was a prisoner at Rome. And the moving spirit in all this good work, we feel safe in saying, was none other than this business woman, Lydia.

5. Lydia, as we have already pointed out, was the first convert to Christ in Europe. Therefore, all that Christianity has done in that great continent had its inception here. This is the fountain. This is the source of the river. That river has since spread over Europe. Not only so, but it has spread over America. It has even flowed into many a foreign land and into the islands of the sea. All the rich blessings of our present Christian civilisation had their beginning here. Therefore, the ultimate outcome of this one conversion was nothing less than the re-making of the world.

IV

There are certainly plain and important lessons here that we all need to remember.

1. There is a lesson for the Christian worker. From this story we learn not to despise the day of small things. It seemed a very trifling service looked at through the eyes of blindness. But to the seeing eye it was one of vast and eternal importance. That seemed like a poor service that an ignorant Methodist layman conducted when he spoke pointedly to a young fellow named Spurgeon. But when he won Spurgeon to Christ, he won a multitude. It seemed of trifling importance when a certain layman spoke to an ignorant

shoe salesman in Boston; but when he won D. L. Moody
to Christ, he pushed two continents up closer to God.

Therefore, let us not despise the day of small things.
You never know when the seemingly insignificant is
going to become the supremely great. Sunday School
teacher, you can never tell just what sowing of yours
is going to result in an abundant harvest. That hour
of patient instruction given to a handful of restless
children may prove to have been the beginning of a
moral revolution. That lesson that in faithfulness
you taught your class of boys may yet mean the dawning of a new day for America or for some distant land
that sits in darkness. We cannot know the importance
of our smallest efforts. We will never know until we
look back upon them from some watchtower in the
Eternal City.

2. There is a precious lesson for the seeker after
God. Are the services in your church a bit dead?
Are the sermons of the preacher or teacher rather mean
deliverances? Keep in the path of duty. Keep your
face turned toward the light. For it is true to-day,
as it was true then, that "if any man is willing to do
His will, he shall know."

VIII

THE MAKING OF A MINISTER—PAUL

The Acts 26:16

"But rise, and stand upon thy feet; for I
have appeared unto thee for this purpose, to
make thee a minister and a witness both of
these things which thou hast seen, and of those
things in the which I will appear unto thee."

I

This is a court scene. The place is the city of
Cesarea, and the time is about A. D. 60. A great con-
course of people has come together in the hall of hearing. There are present the leading citizens of the city
and the ranking officers of the Roman army. King
Agrippa is on the judgment seat. His sister, Bernice,
is at his side, as outwardly fair as she is inwardly
rotten. Paul, the prisoner at the bar, is brought in.
Then Festus opens the proceedings with these words:

"King Agrippa, and all men which are here present with us, ye see this man, about whom all the multitude of the Jews have dealt with me, both at Jerusalem
and also here, crying that he ought not to live any
longer. But when I found that he had committed
nothing worthy of death, and that he himself hath
appealed to Augustus, I have determined to send
him. . . . Wherefore I have brought him forth before
you, and specially before thee, O King Agrippa, that,
after examination had, I might have somewhat to write.

For it seemeth to me unreasonable to send a prisoner and not withal to signify the crimes laid against him."

"Then Agrippa said unto Paul, Thou art permitted to speak for thyself. Then Paul stretched forth the hand and answered for himself." And in this defence Paul accounts for the marvellous change that has been wrought within him. He tells how, more than a quarter of a century ago, life for him had taken on a new purpose. The commission that he had from the Chief Priest had been thrown away and the commission of Jesus Christ had been accepted in its stead. At that time he was changed from a persecutor into a preacher, from a menace into a minister.

II

How was this marvellous change wrought?

Paul is absolutely sure of the answer to that question. It was not wrought by the might of man. It was not brought about by the learning of schools. The worker of this mighty revolution was Jesus Christ. "I heard a voice speaking unto me saying, Saul, Saul, why persecutest thou me? And I said, Who art thou Lord? And He said, I am Jesus, whom thou persecutest. But rise and stand upon thy feet, for I have appeared unto thee for this purpose, to make thee a minister." It was Christ, therefore, that made Paul a minister. And every true minister is so made.

But how did Christ accomplish this high task? Answer: He gave Paul a vision of Himself. Little did Paul dream that day when he set out from Jerusalem to Damascus on his mission of persecution that this wonderful experience would come to him. This, we may say, in spite of the fact that he did not find his self-chosen task of destroying the Church pleasant. He was finding it hard to "kick against the goads." But in spite of this he was keeping up the fight. He was even then nearing the city where he purposed to further redden his hands with Christian blood. Suddenly there was a flash and a fall, and a voice speaking to him. And when he arose to his feet, he was no longer a menace to the Church, but a good minister of Jesus Christ.

III

Now what did this experience do for Paul? How did it fit him for the work of the ministry?

1. It was this vision that made it possible for Christ to give him a new nature. Out on the highway that day Paul was reborn. Out in the glare of that noonday sun he became a new creation. He was lifted upon his feet and made erect by the power of Christ. He became a partaker of the Divine Nature. He passed out of death into life. He was completely transformed. Henceforth he could say in all sincerity and truthfulness: "For to me to live is Christ."

Now since this vision resulted in the remaking of Paul, since it brought him into a personal and saving knowledge of Jesus Christ, it gave him the first and supreme essential for an effective ministry. Certainly nothing could have come to him to take the place of this experience. Without it he would never have preached a single sermon, nor founded a single church, nor won a single soul. And there is absolutely nothing still that will take the place of a like equipment for him who would be a minister. No amount of learning, no amount of eloquence, no amount of personal magnetism can serve as a substitute for the new birth.

The first and fundamental and supreme equipment for the Christian minister is that he experience for himself this mighty transformation that came to Paul that day on the way from Jerusalem to Damascus.

But, mark you, it is not necessary that we enter into this experience in the same way in which Paul entered it. There does not have to be for us a blazing light that flings us prostrate into the dust. Christ may dawn upon us like a sunrise. Or our hearts may open gradually to His incoming as a rosebud opens to full-blown beauty at the kiss of the morning. The conversion of Lydia was far different from that of Paul. She saw no blazing glory. She heard no voice. Yet she was as truly born from above as was the great apostle. The method is not of supreme importance. The fact is the only essential. But every one who aspires to be a true minister of our Lord, whether he serves in pulpit or in pew, must have this absolutely necessary equipment—a personal, saving knowledge of Jesus Christ.

2. This experience gave Paul a compelling motive. Paul had been zealous before his conversion, but his zeal had been for a creed rather than for a person. But the motive power of Paul's life after this experience was not simply a creed, though Paul had a creed. It was love and loyalty to a Person. Had you asked Paul the secret of his ceaseless toil, had you questioned him regarding those daring missionary journeys, he would have answered simply: "The love of Christ constraineth me." What a giver he was! How constantly he was spending and being spent! He ceased not to warn men night and day with tears. His life was a daily dying. What is the secret of this self-giving? Had you asked him the question, this

would have been the answer: "He loved me and gave himself for me."

And this, my brethren, is an essential equipment for every minister. It does not take any great motive to send men on enterprises that cost nothing. It does not take any great motive to enlist us in campaigns that have in them no sweat and no blood. But for those who live lives of constant self-giving, there must be a mighty motive. You may visit the slums with no higher motive than curiosity. But if you live in them in order to redeem them, there must be a motive far more compelling. "Except a corn of wheat fall into the ground and die, it abideth alone." But it takes a motive of mighty potency to make us willing to thus die.

"Why did you become a missionary?" a friend asked Judson one day. "I never thought of that," Mr. Judson replied. But when he had considered the matter for a little while, this was his answer: "I became a missionary because I thought Jesus Christ would be glad to have me become one." He simply wanted to please God. And the reason he wanted to please Him was because he loved Him. There is no other motive so compelling as this. There is none other that will enable us so gladly to give ourselves in sacrificial service morning, noon and night till we reach the goal post at the end of the race.

Not only did this experience bring to Paul love to Christ, it also brought him love to men. After this vision Paul seems to put his arms round the whole world. His heart became a veritable house of many mansions. There were abiding places in it for all sorts and conditions of men. There he gave hospitality to a runaway slave. There he entertained a

demon-possessed girl who followed him through the
streets of Philippi. There he received as guests soldiers and sailors, Jews and Gentiles, ignorant and
educated, bond and free. He loved his friends. He
loved those who were indifferent. He was willing to
spend and be spent for them, though the more he loved
them the less he was loved in return. He loved those
whose faces he had never seen. He loved his enemies.
He did not even refuse hospitality to scornful Agrippa.
"King Agrippa, believest thou the prophets? I know
that thou believest." And King Agrippa is disposed
to sneer: "With a little thou wouldst persuade me to
be a Christian?" And how tender is Paul's answer!
"I would to God that not only thou, but all these that
hear me this day, were both almost and altogether
such as I am, except these bonds." That is love speaking. Paul is saying: "I would not bind you as I
have been bound. But, oh, how gladly, were it in my
power, would I give you my liberating and satisfying
vision of the Lord Jesus Christ."

3. This experience also gave Paul his message.
Here is where Paul found his gospel. He tells the
Galatians very plainly that he did not receive his message from man, but that he received it through the
revelation of God. One day he wrote a letter to the
church at Rome. In this letter is this majestic sentence: "I am not ashamed of the Gospel of Christ,
because it is the power of God unto salvation to every
one that believeth." How had this conviction come
to him? It had come through a personal experience.
He believed that the Gospel was the power of God
unto salvation because he had tested it and found it
true. There was a time when he was not saved. To-
day he is saved. The change has been wrought through

Jesus Christ. Therefore he has a message. Therefore he can call the Gospel my gospel.

We are not to understand, of course, that this one
experience brought Paul all his knowledge of Jesus
Christ. Hear again the word of Christ to him: "Rise
and stand upon thy feet; for I have appeared unto
thee for this purpose, to make thee a minister and a
witness both of these things which thou hast seen, and
of those things in the which I will appear unto thee."
His experience of Christ was a fact of history. It
was a memory of the past. But it was far more than
a memory. It was also a present fact! He was to
witness to what happened yesterday. He was also
to witness to what was happening now and would be
a witness to what would happen to-morrow. He had
a growing experience. His gospel was a growing gospel. His intimacy with Christ was an ever-increasing
intimacy.

But Paul's knowledge of Christ as a personal saviour had its beginning here. Ever after this experience he could say: "I know." And men are waiting
to-day with pathetic heart-hunger for the preacher who
can speak with authority. They are waiting for the
minister who has in his voice a note of absolute certainty. There is no other preaching so gripping, so
arresting, so fascinating as that of the preacher who
has a sure word. There is no other man who helps
us so much as the one that comes into the pulpit to
tell what he has found true in his own personal experience. He may lack education, he may lack ability,
he may lack polish, but if he has assurance, he will
not be lacking in usefulness. Let him be able to say,
"Here is the road that I took and it led me unto the
heights. Here is the rock to which I clung in the

storm, and I found it to be the Rock of Ages," and the hearts of the saints will be comforted, and the careless crowd will be won to a vital faith.

This accounts for the effective preaching of that outcast woman that met Jesus at the well. Had you seen her as she hurried into the city you might have asked her purpose. Suppose she had shouted at you as she hurried on, "I am going into Sychar to preach Jesus." How astonished you would have been! When you had recovered from the shock enough to speak, you might have shouted after her: "You going to preach, you who are nothing more than a filthy piece of human driftwood! You going to preach, and to a crowd that knows the story of your soiled and ragged life!" And you might even have laughed in scorn. But in spite of all her defects, and they seemed sufficient to make her mission utterly hopeless, we read this: "Many believed because of the saying of the woman."

Why did this woman win? It was not because of her unclean past. She won in spite of that. She won because she could speak with assurance. And, my brethren, if we are to preach effectively, we must see to it each for himself that the Gospel becomes "my gospel." We must know something of the saving power of Jesus Christ in our own personal lives. Having experienced this, then let us tell a doubting, questioning, troubled world what we ourselves have tested and found true. Let us be silent about our uncertainties and speak of our certainties. Let us be silent for a while about the things of which we are not sure and tell the things of which we are sure. Let us leave off the discussion of what we do not know and tell of what we do know. Men are hungry for a sure word, and when they hear it they will not hear in vain.

IV

But how was this vision that came to Paul able to work this great change in his life?

We sometimes feel that there was a bit of compulsion in it. We feel that if only such a vision should come to us, we too would be entirely re-made. But this vision in itself did not re-make Paul. What, then, was the secret of its transforming power? It was this: Paul responded to it. Here is his joyful declaration: "Whereupon, O King Agrippa, I was not disobedient unto the heavenly vision."

Paul might have disobeyed. Millions have done so. He might have turned from this vision to utter moral blindness. That has been the history of multitudes. You can treat the truth in such a fashion as to make it untrue to you. You can so rebel against the light as to turn it into darkness. You can refuse to see till you lose your capacity to see. The secret of the transforming power of this vision was that Paul then and there became obedient. "Who art thou, Lord?" he cries while prostrate in the dust. As yet he is uncertain about many things, but of this at least he is sure: the One who has appeared unto him is henceforth his Lord. He puts himself absolutely at His disposal. He surrenders to Him unconditionally. Henceforth he stands ready to give up all things to which Jesus objects. Henceforth he stands ready to undertake all tasks to which He calls. But for that act of personal surrender, Paul, the gospel minister and missionary, would never have existed.

And the conditions are not different for ourselves. All visions are of no avail, all knowledge about Christ comes to naught unless we ourselves are obedient. We must enthrone Jesus Christ as our Lord. We must give ourselves in unconditional surrender to Him. If we do this He will accept us. If we do this He will use us. Some He will send into the pulpit, some He will send into the uttermost parts of the earth. Every one He will use somewhere. For He delights to give "to every man his work." Only let us come to Him! Only let us fling ourselves in utter abandon before Him, and He will speak to us the word He spoke to Paul: "Rise and stand upon thy feet; for I have appeared unto thee for this purpose, to make thee a minister and a witness both of these things which thou hast seen, and of those things in the which I will appear unto thee."

IX

A NOBLE BOAST—PAUL

I Corinthians 1 : 22-23

"The Jews require a sign, and the Greeks
seek after wisdom; but we preach Christ crucified, unto the Jews a stumbling block and unto
the Greeks foolishness, but unto them which
are called, both Jews and Greeks, Christ the
power of God, and the wisdom of God."

We call your special attention to a part of the
twenty-third verse: "We preach Christ crucified." This
is an autobiographical touch. Paul is speaking out
of his own experience. And it will be well worth our
while to listen to him, for he is truly great. I doubt
if any other single individual has ever influenced the
human race as he has influenced it. During his own
lifetime he touched and produced moral revolutions
in two continents. Even his enemies said of him that
he had turned the world upside down. More than
eighteen centuries have passed since he lived. Civilisa-
tions that flourished then are now no more. Thrones
have toppled down and crowns have rotted in heaps.
But this man's influence instead of diminishing has
only increased with the years. To-day if he were here
he might say once again: "I press toward the mark
for the prize." For his days of greatest power are
yet ahead.

I

What is his secret? What did he to influence the
world so mightily? What did he to enrich the moral
life of the world?

It is said that Napoleon lowered the stature of the
manhood of France by one inch. But here is a Christ-
conquered Jew who has marvellously increased the
moral stature of the race. How did he do it? When
he accounts for himself here in this text he does so
by saying: "We preach." His work was the work of
the ministry. His highest claim for himself was that of
being a preacher of the Gospel of Christ.

"We preach." And, mark you, the word "preach"
as here used does not carry the idea of theorising or
of wordy discussion. "We preach" means we proclaim,
we deliver a message not our own, but one that was
delivered to us. We preach, we enunciate, we assert,
we declare. Paul was evidently a positive preacher.
He was emphatic. He did not deal in mere doubts and
interrogations. He did not come to peddle out proba-
bilities. He spoke to men the revelations that had
come to himself. That he called preaching. He had
a right so to call it, and I think I have a right to say
that nothing else is, in the true sense, preaching.

II

No doubt there were times when Paul was tempted
to do something other than preach. There was great
demand among his hearers for something else.

1. The Jews were constantly demanding signs. That
is, they wanted physical and visible demonstrations of
the truth. They wanted to witness miracles, wonders.

This eagerness for signs is with us still. It expresses itself to-day in our love for ritualism. As we lose a sense of the invisible Christ we seek to atone for the loss by outward show and splendour. When they have taken away our Lord, we try to content our souls with creeds and candles and crucifixes. Then the passion of the sign seeker shows itself in another way. We find it in the greediness for physical cures such as those claimed by the Christian Scientist. We want an eye and ear demonstration of the fact of immortality, such as the Spiritualist is constantly seeking and oftentimes fooling himself into believing that he has found.

But the tragedy of all this sign seeking is that there is in it no saving power. It does not conquer sin. It does not make us holy. It does not transform us into the image of Christ. "A wicked and adulterous generation seeketh after a sign." And after all their seeking and maybe finding, they remained wicked and adulterous. Paul knew this. Hence he refused to turn aside from the work of preaching to that of the giving or working of signs.

2. Paul was no doubt tempted at times to satisfy the hunger of the Greek after wisdom. The Greek loved elaborate philosophies. He was fond of rhetoric and oratory. He revelled in eloquence and happy epigrams. He admired cleverness. He was a worshipper of intellect. He prostrated himself before genius. And whenever a congregation begins to seek first in its minister mere human wisdom, whenever you come to hear a man simply because he is clever, you are not on your way to salvation. This Paul knew. So he refused to be diverted even by worldly wisdom from his high task of preaching.

III

What was the theme of Paul's preaching?

He did not give himself up to a discussion of the themes of the forum or of the market place. He did not give over his hour of opportunity to commenting on the latest scandal or crime that had been committed in Corinth. "We preach Christ." His was the gospel of a Person. He was a man of vast powers, but he believed that here was a theme worthy of his most intense efforts, worthy of all the powers of his gigantic intellect.

"We preach Christ." Note the word. He does not say, "We preach about Christ." Anybody can do that. A preacher who has lost his vision, whose heart has grown cold, into whose voice the metallic has crept, can talk about Christ. A dead Sunday School teacher can preach about Him. Even a backslidden and lifeless church member can preach about Christ. In fact the rankest atheist might do the same. Many of them do. It is almost fashionable for folks who do not accept Christ to speak flatteringly about Him. But Paul does not claim simply to talk about Christ. What he says is: "We preach Christ."

Now there is only one man who can do that and that is the man who knows Christ, the man who has opened the door of his heart for the incoming of Christ. That is the man who can say: "I am crucified with Christ; nevertheless I live, and yet not I, but Christ liveth in me." When Paul opened his lips Christ spoke through them. That was the secret of his power. That is the secret of the power of every really effective preacher. I shall bless and help you to-day only as Christ has right-of-way in my own heart. If He speaks

through my own blundering lips, then even I shall
have "a mouth and a wisdom that the world cannot
gainsay nor resist."

Not only does Paul preach Christ, but Christ crucified. This does not mean that every sermon that Paul
preached dealt with the crucifixion of Jesus. It does
mean that every sermon that he preached had as its
fountain a suffering and dying Saviour. Had he
merely preached Christ as a great teacher or as the
world's ideal man, he would have given very little
offence. Neither would he have wrought any great
revolutions. Neither would there have been anything
wonderfully new or revolutionary in his message. But
the theme of his preaching was this: "Christ crucified."

IV

Why did Paul cling to this theme through all the
stormy and stressful days of his ministry?

He did not do so because the theme was universally
popular. It was not. One night he saw a vision of
a man of Macedonia who was stretching out eager
hands and calling for help. But when he hurried to
the rescue he met no flattering reception. He had only
been in the city of Philippi a very few days when
he found himself with torn garments and a bleeding
body in the inner precincts of a Roman prison. Released from there he went to Thessalonica, where lewd
fellows of the baser sort again raised the mob against
him. Thence he fled to Berea, thence to Athens and
now he is in Corinth. Everywhere he has gone his
message has aroused scorn and hatred and opposition.

Arrived in Corinth there seems no doubt that he

was for a while sorely tempted to keep silent. Preaching seemed so futile. Its whole result, he felt tempted to believe, was to awaken the scorn and anger and contempt and hatred of the people. "I was with you in weakness and in fear and much trembling." And it required a special vision from the Lord to set him preaching again. They had called him a babbler over in Athens. But God said to him now: "Babble on and hold not your peace, for I have much people in this city." And so he took up his task of preaching Christ crucified, but it was not at the call of popularity.

Neither did Paul preach Christ crucified because it was all that he knew. Paul was a scholar. He was a man of profound intellect. He was familiar with Greek culture and Greek thought. He knew quite well that he had it in his power to win these contemptuous Greeks. He knew he could bring them to his feet in profound admiration. On Mars' Hill he had talked the vernacular of Greek philosophers as if he had been born and bred in Athens. But the results had been disappointing. So he refused to cater further to this love of wisdom. It cost him a battle, for he was human. But here is his declaration of independence: "I determined not to know anything among you save Christ and Him crucified."

Paul persistently preached Christ crucified for the following reasons: Because he was fully persuaded that it was this message and this alone that was sufficient adequately to meet the needs of our lost and ruined race. He believed this because it is through Christ crucified and through Him alone that we can come to really know God, His nature and His thought of ourselves.

1. Christ crucified is a revelation of the holiness of God. The Jews had conceived of God as holy before Christ died. Isaiah had seen angels veil their faces in His presence and cry, "Holy, holy, holy is the Lord of hosts." But even this is not the deepest revelation of the holiness of God. The deepest revelation of His holiness is God suffering and dying in the person of Jesus Christ to redeem man from the curse of sin.

2. Through Christ crucified we come to understand God's hatred of sin. Sin is such a trivial matter to many of us. We say, "It will all come out in the wash." Or, "It will not matter a hundred years from now." How we are suffering to-day from a cheap idea of sin! What we need for the correction of this terrible and tragic ignorance is a vision of Christ crucified. If it seems a small matter to you to sin, it is because you know nothing of Him who sweat bloody sweat under the trees of Gethsemane. You have never seen Him of the thorn-crowned brow. You have never come into vital touch with Him who cried on the cross: "My God! My God! Why hast thou forsaken me?" Christ crucified is God's eternal heartache because of your sin and mine.

3. Through Christ crucified God reveals to us his estimate of man. What does God think of the moral condition of man? I am not asking how modern scholars think of him. I am not asking what we ourselves think. We may think of ourselves as very decent and respectable. We may think of ourselves as rich and increased in goods and in need of nothing. But God's thought of man is different. He says we are wretched and miserable and poor and blind and naked. He says: "There is no difference: for all sinned and come short

of the glory of God." You cannot understand the cross except in the light of the lostness of man.

But just as firm as is God's conviction of the lostness of man, just so firm is His faith in his salvability. He dares to speak to the most hopeless of us this amazing word: "Be ye perfect even as your Father which is in heaven is perfect." He believes that the worst man in Jericho is a possible son of Abraham. He believes that the fluctuating son of Jona can become a rock of Christ-like character. He believes that even a dying robber can be made into a saint fit to companion Himself in Paradise. Therefore, just as clearly as the cross reveals God's belief in the lostness of man, just so clearly does it reveal His faith in man's perfectability.

Some one tells this story: Over in Scotland a few years ago a charming young girl discovered that a trestle had been washed away on a certain line of railroad. She hurried down the track to meet the oncoming express. She met it in a narrow defile. She flagged the train, but lost her life. At one end of that train there was a deep, yawning chasm. At the other end there was the mangled body of the girl. Now the only adequate explanation of this mangled body at the rear of the train is the yawning chasm in front. And the only intelligible explanation of the cross of Jesus Christ is the terrible chasm into which man's sin has plunged him and the possibility of his being rescued from that doom.

4. In Christ crucified we see love bringing a remedy for man's sin. Paul had no doubt of the lostness of man. Just as little did he doubt the power of Christ crucified to remake man. He was not ashamed of

the Gospel because it was the power of God unto salvation. This he knew as a matter of personal experience. This he knew in the deepest recesses of his own soul. He declared with the profoundest conviction that Christ crucified was the power of God, because he had experienced that power in his own life. So satisfying was that experience that we hear him shout: "God forbid that I should glory, save in the cross of our Lord Jesus crucified; whereby the world has been crucified unto me and I unto the world."

v

Brethren, all our needs are met in Him. No wonder Paul clung to this gospel. He knew it to be fully adequate to his own needs and to the needs of the whole world. It is said that some years ago an engineer was driving an excursion train up a grade some miles west of Altoona, Pennsylvania. He looked up the track and saw four freight cars loaded with stone that had broken loose from the engine and were coming at a terrific rate down the grate. He ordered the fireman to go back and stand on the platform of the baggage car and uncouple the cars from his engine and let them drift down the grade, while he should go alone to meet the oncoming cars. He met them and they were ditched. When they dragged his mangled body from under the heap of scrap iron that had once been an engine, he said: "What! nobody hurt? Thank God, I turned the trick."

We are not here to give you any elaborate theory of the atonement. But this we assert: Christ has gone alone to meet our enemy and He has met him and His victory is complete and overwhelming. So that we can confidently say: "He was wounded for our transgressions; He was bruised for our iniquities; the chastisement of our peace was upon Him, and with His stripes we are healed."

What will you do with this salvation that is offered to you in Jesus Christ? Those who heard of it from the lips of St. Paul did not all accept it. To some it was only a stumbling block. To others it was mere foolishness. They went on seeking for signs. They went on worshipping at the shrine of wisdom. But those who did accept, those who believed the message found it true. They found that Christ crucified was indeed the power of God. And so may you this day. Therefore, with joy I take these brave words upon my lips: "But we preach Christ crucified, unto the Jews a stumbling block, and unto the Greeks foolishness; but unto them which are called, both Jews and Greeks, Christ the power of God and the wisdom of God."

X

THE WASTE BASKET—PAUL

Philippians 3 : 13-14

"This one thing I do, forgetting those things which are behind, and reaching forth unto those things which are before, I press toward the mark for the prize."

Whatever you may think of my message you will at least agree that I have a great text. It is a text that lets us into the secret of one of the most majestic and useful lives that was ever lived on this planet. Paul, though poor, made many rich in the far-off day in which he lived. And he has been at the big business of distributing spiritual legacies all through the centuries. How many multi-millionaires here and in heaven owe their success under God to him! And how did it all come about? A bit of the secret is in the text: "This one thing I do, forgetting those things which are behind, and reaching forth unto those things which are before, I press toward the mark for the prize."

1. From this text we learn that Paul was a specialist. Paul was not bent upon a dozen different enterprises. He was not even engaged in two. He was giving all his time, all his attention, all his vast abilities to one single task. "This one thing I do." And, mark you, life becomes mighty only as all its energies are concentrated upon the doing of one thing. Recently I saw a mountainside being removed by hy-

108

draulic pressure. When that water fell from the clouds
it had a greater height to give it power. Yet even
then so softly did it fall that it would not have hurt
the tender face of a baby. But there was that same
water with sufficient force to move mountains. Why?
It was concentrated. It could say, "This one thing I
do."

2. Not only was Paul a man of one single purpose, but that purpose was one that was altogether
worthy. If Paul staked everything upon one single
adventure, it was an adventure that was genuinely
worth while. "This one thing I do." What was
that one thing? To what end was he striving?
To what end was he battling every hour and every
day and every year of his eventful and fruitful life?
This is his answer: "That I may lay hold of that for
which I was laid hold of by Jesus Christ." And Paul
is back again to that marvellous experience that came
to him on the way from Jerusalem to Damascus. That
day Christ arrested him. He laid hold of him. And
this Christ did for a definite purpose. Christ arrested
Paul that day for Paul's salvation. That day he became a new creation in Christ Jesus.

But Christ meant more in this arresting of Paul
than his own salvation. "Rise and stand upon thy
feet: for I have appeared unto thee for this purpose,
to make thee a minister and a witness both of these
things which thou hast seen and of those things in the
which I will appear unto thee." Christ not only purposed the remaking of Paul. He purposed the making
of Paul into a minister. He saved him that he might
become His witness. He transformed him in order
that through him He might bring this saving and
transforming Gospel to others. Day by day he sought

to bring himself more fully to conform to the will of God. Day by day he gave himself to spend and be spent in the service of others.

3. Not only did Paul set himself to one high purpose, but he went about the achieving of that purpose in a most wise and intelligent fashion. He made the best possible use of his waste basket. He knew what things to throw away and what things to keep. We all have our waste baskets. Now and then it is necessary to go through the desk where letters and papers of various kinds accumulate and sort out what is worth keeping and throw the rest into the waste basket. Unless we clean things up now and then, the desk becomes so littered that it is next to impossible for us to do our work. There are a great many things that need to be thrown away. There are also many things that need to be kept. Happy is the man who knows how to use his waste basket wisely.

I

Watch Paul use his. "Forgetting those things which are behind." This does not mean that Paul forgot everything that was behind. He did not blot out his past altogether and leave it a perfect blank. That would have been at once an impossibility and a colossal misfortune. There were some things that Paul kept. There were some things of yesterday that he did not dare throw away. There are some things that you dare not throw away.

1. If in searching through the desk of last year you come across any unpaid bills, do not tear them up and throw them in the waste basket. That is what some do. But that is not Paul's way. It is not the

way of righteousness and fairness. Last year you got
hard put to it financially. You asked your friend for
a loan. He granted it. That is behind you now, but
do not forget it. Do not forget that bill that you owe
the grocery man just because you have eaten the gro-
ceries. Do not forget the pledge that you made to the
Church just because you made it last year. Do not
forget the vow that you made to God, the pledge of
a new service and of a new loyalty. It is exceedingly
easy to forget these things. But they must not be
forgotten. To forget them is to deal a death blow to
our honesty.

2. Do not forget the wrongs that you inflicted last
year, which wrongs you might right if you desired.
Do not forget the apology that you ought to make.
Do not forget the wound you made that it is your duty
to heal. For God not only expects us to stop doing
the wrong; He expects us to right the wrong so far as
it is in our power. You will never find peace so long
as you cling to that which is not rightfully yours.
You will never enter into the joy of your Lord so
long as you refuse to make right that injustice that was
wrought by your hands.

A few years ago Gypsy Smith was holding a meeting in Chicago. A very wealthy old bachelor who was
a member of a prominent church attended the services.
Gypsy Smith preached a sermon on restitution. That
sermon brought home to the conscience of this wealthy
bachelor a great sin committed in the hot-blooded days
of his youth. A woman had been wronged by him.
She slept now in a distant grave. But there were two
children, a boy and a girl. They had been put in an
orphans' asylum. That wealthy bachelor went for these
children and found that the girl had died. But the

boy he brought to his palatial home in the city. As they sat together the first night he said to the lad: "Son, do you think you could ever love your father, though he did your mother a great wrong?" And the boy said, "I do not know." "Do you think you could ever be happy here in the city?" Again he said, "I do not know." Then the man said, "Would you like to see your father?" The boy looked wistful for a moment and then said that he would. Then the man said, "Put your arms around my neck and call me father." And that man testified that he found Jesus Christ through the clinging arms of his son. Do not forget your un-righted wrong. God has not forgotten and you must not.

3. Paul is not asking us to forget the kindnesses that have been shown us during the year past. Do not forget the flowers that were sent to you when your heart was heavy. Do not forget the sympathy that helped to dry your tears when you were in the midst of great grief. Do not forget the encouraging word that was spoken by a friend when you were weak and faltering and ready to fall. Do not forget the hand that steadied you when your feet were about to stagger out of the path. If somebody has been a blessing to you, it is well to carry the memory of that fact with you into the new year. That was Paul's way. "The Lord give mercy unto the house of Onesiphorus, for he often refreshed me and was not ashamed of my chain."

4. Do not forget the mercy of God that came to you last year. Paul was the last one who would have urged upon us that we forget the blessings that are behind us. Again and again he was going back to that great event when his soul had its birthday. He was

always thanking because he was thinking so constantly
of past mercies. And if we would not fling away real
treasure, let us carry the memory of God's mercies with
us into the year that is ahead.

II

But there are some things that we can afford to
throw away. There are some things, in fact, that we
must throw into the waste basket or we shall be seriously hampered. We must part with these things or
the chances are we shall make no progress at all.

1. I would advise that you throw away whatever
wrongs you may have suffered last year. Why keep
them? They do not help you in the least. Did somebody write you a love letter? Keep that. Did somebody write you a word of appreciation? File it away
and some day when the rain is on the roof get it out
and read it. It will help you. But why keep the
other kind? I went into the office the other day to
find the most bitter and scathing letter that I have
ever read. Do you know what I did with it? I tore
it up very quickly and put it into the waste basket.
Why keep it? I would not mind keeping a butterfly,
but why pet a snake? It is worth while to cultivate
roses. But why give your time to the cultivation of
nettles?

Has somebody injured you, deceived you, cheated
you, done you a great wrong? Forget it. For if you
remember it the memory of it will harden into hate.
Hate will be changed into cynicism. You will become
bitter, antagonistic, disillusioned. Of course you may
get even with the one who wronged you. You may
succeed in getting revenge. But while you make him

suffer, you yourself will suffer the pangs of hell. You remember Silent Kate in "The Light in the Clearing." Silent Kate was grievously, horribly, hideously wronged. A man whom she loved wrecked her life and threw her away. Kate gave the rest of her years to an effort for revenge. She won. She saw the son of her enemy die on the scaffold. She saw the enemy himself die of a broken heart. But her triumph was only the bitterest disaster. Her success had in it the sting of a million fiery serpents. Therefore if you love happiness, if you yearn for the sunshine, if you covet a bit of springtime in your soul, throw away hate. Cast out all your grudges. You can find peace in no other way. "Forgive us our sins as we forgive those who sin against us." Christ cannot forgive you unless you forgive others. He cannot because His forgiveness means not simply the remission of a penalty, but it means a new heart. But He cannot give you a new heart when you cling tenaciously to the old.

2. As you enter into to-morrow you can afford to throw away the record of your past failures and blunders and mistakes. You made a terrible failure last year. You made a mistake that you feel will cast a shadow over all your to-morrows. What are you doing about it? I can tell you what not to do. Do not keep your eyes fixed upon it. Do not be guilty of the tragic blunder of trying to break through the door of the past and live it over again. You cannot do that. Do not allow it so to unnerve you and discourage you as to keep you from doing anything with the present.

A few weeks ago a mother came to see me. She was one of the most broken-hearted women I ever met. Her boy had gone wrong. He had committed a crime.

She felt that his going wrong was due in large measure to herself. She realised that she had failed. But instead of turning her back upon her failure and setting herself to do the best with to-morrow, she declared that she would never try again. She declared in her bitterness that never again would she pray. Never again would she open God's Word. Never again would she enter God's house. She allowed her yesterday to utterly rob her of her to-day and of her to-morrow.

But Paul's word to her, Paul's word to you, is to forget the tragic mistake and failure of yesterday. To always be gazing upon it will make it no less a mistake. It will only palsy your hand and take the courage out of your soul. That was a terrible failure that the disciples made when they went into Gethsemane to watch with Jesus. They failed to watch. They went to sleep. They slept till the Son of Man was betrayed into the hands of sinners. But what said Jesus to them even after this horrible failure? He said: "Rise up; let us be going." If yesterday was a failure, there is but one thing to do with it. Forget it. Tear it up as you would a worthless piece of scrap paper and throw it into the waste basket.

3. Then there is your old sin. Yesterday you sinned. What are you going to do about that grim fact? Maybe all last year you spent in sin. What is to be done with all the scarlet stains that are upon your soul? What is to be done with all the foul pages written into your life's story? What is to be done with sin, the sin of last year, the sin of the years past? The answer to this question may startle you. Forget it. Turn your back upon it through faith in Christ. For God Himself forgets it. "He will forgive your transgressions

and remember them no more." If you are trusting in Jesus this morning He has forgotten that you ever sinned. Every sin that you have ever committed He has blotted out of the book of His remembrance. And what God forgets you have a right to forget.

4. Paul forgot himself. As we enter into the New Year it would be well for us to forget ourselves. Is not the biggest tragedy of our lives just this: that we are self-centred rather than God-centred? We live within our own wills instead of within His will. Is it not true that this has been the source of our wrongdoing, of our heartache, of our failure, of our loss of opportunities? But if we are trusting Christ today, the old life of self is to be forgotten. "For ye are dead, and your life is hid with Christ in God." So as we pass out of the old into the new, let us forget self. Victory will come in no other way.

III

'And why does Paul forget the things that are behind? Why does he urge us to forget? For the simple reason that he knows we will never run forward when our eyes are turned backward. If you are constantly looking in the past, looking at past sins and failures, you will never go forward. Men walk in the direction in which they look. And if you have the backward look this morning, you also have the backward step. It is only as we turn our eyes to the future, to the things that are before that we will make progress. The backward look means loss. It means we shall stand death-smitten and petrified, as did Lot's wife when she looked back at the burning city.

IV

But you say, "That is all well enough. But how can I forget?" Yes, that is the question—How? And let me tell you frankly that you will not forget by simply trying to do so. You will never succeed in this great undertaking by simply saying, "Now, go to. I am going to forget." I remember a man I met years ago who was resolved to forget. He said he had to. But he could not. He went on remembering and remembering in spite of himself. He tried to dodge memory, but he could not. He tried to out-run it, but he found it impossible. At last he went stark mad because he could not forget.

How can I forget the things that are behind? There is only one way and that is by becoming absorbed in the things that are before. Do you remember that first love affair of yours? or can you remember back that far? You felt that it was going to be fatal. You were sure that you would marry. But she went away and you forgot her. How did it come about? You became interested in somebody else. You forgot one by remembering another. That is the way Paul forgot his yesterday. He became absorbed in the things of to-day and to-morrow.

How did Silas Marner lose his love for gold? Not by having his gold stolen. He loved it just as well after it was gone, possibly even better, than he did before. But one night when he came home he saw something on the hearth that scintillated and sparkled in the flare of the fire somewhat as his gold used to do. Eagerly he rushed forward with the hope that his gold had come back. But as he gripped this sparkling something with his miserly fingers, he found that it was not gold, but the silken tresses of a little lost child. Eppie slipped into his heart and filled it so full of tender, new, human love that he forgot his love for gold.

Do you remember the Jackal in "The Tale of Two Cities"? What an unlovely and self-centred and repellent personality was Sydney Carton! But one day he forgot himself. And in that noble forgetfulness he slipped into a prison cell. He took another man's place at the guillotine. And those who saw him die said his face was the most peaceful face upon which they had ever looked. How did he manage to forget himself? By remembering somebody else. He lost his self-love in the love of another. And so we are to forget self by giving our heart's love to Christ and to our brethren for Christ's sake.

v

"Forgetting the things which are behind and reaching forth unto those things which are before"—that is the only way we can become emancipated from the past. That is the only way we can achieve our present and our future. We must become absorbed in the things that are before. And what are some of those things? I know there is much that is lovely that lies behind us. But what are some of the things that are ahead of us this morning that still make life worth living, that make the hilltops ahead golden with blessed possibilities?

1. Jesus Christ is still ahead of us. You rejected Him last year maybe. But you have not run past Him yet. He was in yesterday, but, thank God, He is in

to-day and will be in to-morrow. "He is the same yesterday, to-day and forever." But though Christ was in yesterday, you cannot find Him there. But you can find Him in to-day and you can walk with Him to-morrow. Christ is ahead. So you have Him to look forward to as you turn your back upon the past. And He says to you just what He said to His disciples who failed Him as you failed Him: "Rise up; let us be going."

2. Eternity is ahead of you. Many here are no longer in the springtime of life. Our hair is growing grey. Our strength is failing and we say, "Few and evil have been the days of the years of my pilgrimage." Some of us have spent the best part of our lives in sin. There may be some who have spent all their lives up to this hour in sin. What have I to say to you? Just this: Eternity is yet ahead of you. "Yes, but I have wasted so much. I can never be the same again." I know. But though you have wasted many a precious day, there is yet as much time ahead of you as there is ahead of God Himself. If God can only wake you up and get you started, blessedness undreamed of is yet possible for you. You have a whole eternity yet on your hands. And what a wonderful man you may become among the tall sons of the morning if you will only begin! If you have only one more minute to live in this world, still I say, eternity is ahead of you. Lay hold of this heartening fact and you will start even yet to press toward the mark for the prize.

3. If you will dare to begin, perfection is ahead of you. However warped and bent and broken and unsightly you are at this moment, however stained and tarnished, however eaten and disfigured by the leprosy of sin, yet perfection is ahead of you if you will only

claim it. For that is His own promise. "We know not what we shall be, but we know that when He shall appear we shall be like Him; for we shall see Him as He is."

4. Home is ahead of us. Where is your home? If you mean the home of your childhood, it exists only in the yesterday. In the drawer of my desk I have a photograph. It is the picture of the home of my childhood. It is about all that is left of it, except an old ruin and many a precious memory. It can never be what it once was. That I know beyond a peradventure. Childhood's home is in the past. It has slipped out beyond my reach. There is absolutely no road that leads to the old front gate and the front porch where Mother used to wait when we came home from school.

Yet, though that is gone, our real home is ahead. "Let not your heart be troubled. Ye believe in God, believe also in me. In my father's house are many mansions. If it were not so I would have told you. I go to prepare a place for you; and if I go and prepare a place for you, I will come again and receive you unto myself, that where I am there ye may be also." Thank God that blessed experience is not behind us. It is in this home that we shall find our finest friendships. It is in this home that we shall lock arms with those whom we "have loved long since and lost awhile." Therefore, let us say with Paul this last Sunday of the old year, "This one thing I do, forgetting those things which are behind, and reaching forth unto those things which are before, I press toward the mark for the prize."

XI

THE GIVER—PETER

Acts 3:6

"Silver and gold have I none, but such as I
have give I thee."

I

These are the words of Simon Peter. He is speaking to a certain beggar who has asked him for alms.
In reply to this beggar's appeal Peter said: "I have
neither silver nor gold, nevertheless I give." These
last two words, "I give," have an autobiographical
flavour. They give in some measure an epitome of
Peter's life. In them he tells the task at which he
toils morning, noon and night. In them he tells what
it means to him to live and what it has meant ever
since his meeting with Jesus. What is Peter's work?
It is giving. He can sum up his whole biography
since he became a follower of Christ in these two short
words, "I give."

Now the story we have before us is a good illustra-
tion of this fact. Peter's encounter with the beggar
is a picture of a typical day in his life. Not that
Peter did the same things every day. Not that he was
every day made the agent through whom God worked
miracles. But Peter was actuated always by the same
passion. He was dominated always by the same spirit.

His passion was not that of getting, it was not that of winning fame or fortune, it was not that of achieving greatness in the eyes of men. The one white hot passion of his life was that of giving. His ambition was to be able to say, "I give."

Look at the story. It is the prayer meeting hour. At least that is the hour that had struck for Peter and his friend John. That hour has not struck for some of us yet. The prayer meeting hour is one that never comes in the calendar of most folks. It is an hour that is not to be found even in the calendar of most church members. Do you happen to know a more lifeless service than the ordinary prayer meeting? Do you know of any service that is more trying to the pastor, that is often more pathetic in its grave-like chill and deadness? How often have I heard some discouraged saint thank God that where two or three were gathered together there was He in the midst? But there was no thrill in the prayer because the one who uttered it was not half so much moved by the joyful sense of the Divine presence as by an oppressing sense of the human absence.

When the hour came for the prayer meeting Peter turned his feet toward the house of God. There are those who possess his wisdom still. When other church members have gone to the show or have gone to sleep or have gone to the dance, these find their way to the place of prayer. Thank God for the large number in our own church who have this as their custom. We have one of the best attended prayer meetings in America. But in all frankness I am not giving the credit for this to some of you who hear me. I am not giving the credit for this to some of the officials of the church. You have never made the slightest con-

tribution toward making the prayer meeting a success.
If everybody had treated it as you have, it would be
so dead that it would make a funeral vault look like
a street carnival.

Peter went to prayer meeting. And this he did in
spite of the fact that he was a very busy man. In
all probability he had been much engaged in religious
work during the morning hours of this very day. Possibly he had preached and had seen thousands of souls
brought into the Kingdom. But in spite of the fact
that he was busy, in spite of the fact that God had
used him to preach to great multitudes, in spite of the
fact that He had honoured him by allowing him to
win great numbers to Jesus Christ, yet he was not too
busy to attend prayer meeting.

Not only did this busy man go to prayer meeting,
but he went in spite of the fact that the meeting to
which he went was doubtless a rather tame and uninteresting affair. But Peter is not going simply for
what he can get. He is going for what he can give.
"Peter, it is a dry desert of a service into which you
are going." And he replies: "I ought to be there,
for my Master has said that if we believe on Him,
out of our inner lives shall flow rivers of living water.
Maybe I can help turn the desert into a garden." "It
is a dead service," I tell him. But he answers: "If
it is dead, it is all the more necessary that I go. Maybe
I can bring some life into it. The more impoverished
a service is, the more necessary it becomes that I go.
If there were all the light and warmth and joy and
power in it that there ought to be, then my presence
would not be so needful, but since so much is wanting,
my presence is absolutely necessary."

Now it was while Peter was on his way to this service

that he came face to face with his great opportunity. Since he was eager to give he was seeking an opportunity to give. Since he was eager to help his eyes were wide open for a chance to help. And it is ever true here as elsewhere that "he that seeketh findeth." Peter's opportunity came in the person of a beggar. This beggar did not mean opportunity to every one. To some he meant only a pest, a nuisance, a parasite. But to Peter he meant an opportunity to give.

This beggar did not ask for much. He would have been well satisfied with a penny. Peter would have been glad enough to have given him a penny if he had only had one. But when this apostle searched his pockets he found that he did not have a cent. So he turns to this beggar and tells him frankly that he has not a penny in the world. "Silver and gold have I none." And having said this, we expect to see him hurry on into the temple, telling John meantime how glad he would have been to have given him something if he had only had as much money as some Crœsus of their acquaintance. But Peter did not do this. Instead, he said: "I have neither silver nor gold, but what I have, I give."

II

What did Peter give?

He did not give money. He had none. He did not give this man a position. He had no position at his disposal. He did not give him an education. That was beyond Peter's power. He gave him simply what he had, not what he expected to have to-morrow, nor what he had yesterday, but that which was a possession of his at that moment. "What I have I give."

Now, since Peter gave what he had and only that, we cannot but realise that the very poorest of us may do as well as he. This great apostle could do nothing bigger nor better than give what he had. But the very least of all can do that well. Every man can be a giver. We may be failures financially. We may be physical failures. We may spend our best years in the sick roof fisticuffing with death. We may not be greatly gifted intellectually. We may have but few educational advantages. We may be devoid of all musical talent. But in spite of all difficulties, in spite of all weaknesses, we can give. Every man can be a giver if he wants to be.

And giving is a privilege. It is blessed to receive; it is good to watch the parched earth receive the rain after a long drought. It is good to watch the dew-drenched world receive the sun's kiss when night is gone. It is good to see a man open his hands and heart to receive God's gifts. But, according to Christ, "it is more blessed to give than to receive." It is more blessed because it is more Godlike. Giving is the task at which God works from eternity to eternity. The very heart of the Gospel is this: "God so loved the world that He gave." And when we are at our best we also long to give. "Not to taste sweet things, but to do true and noble things and to vindicate ourselves under God's heaven as God-made men and women, is that for which every son of Adam dimly longs."

Now, because every man may give, it is every man's duty to give. To refuse to give is to refuse to live. There are two seas with which we are familiar in the Bible story. One of these seas looked out one morning and saw a delightful visitor coming. It was the River Jordan. And when it came singing and shimmering

and laughing, the little sea of Galilee was glad. It
opened wide its arms and took the gracious river to its
heart and kissed it on the lips and said, "Precious gift,
you are too good to keep."

"The dry fields burn and the mills are to turn,
And a myriad flowers mortally yearn."

And so it passed the river on to others.

And there was another sea and it looked out and
saw this same river coming. And it too was glad. It also
gave the river welcome. But once it had taken it into
its arms it held it fast and said: "It's mine, all mine.
I will not give a drop for the watering of the rose's
petal or for the moistening of the lips of a fevered
child." And that day this sea put on its shroud. And
that day it slipped into its coffin. And that day the
laws of nature, which are the laws of God, said above
that sea, "Earth to earth; ashes to ashes; dust to dust."
And we know this sea to-day by the name of the Dead
Sea. For "he that saveth his life shall lose it." To
give is to live. To refuse to give is to die. Peter
found life instead of death by being able to say: "I
give."

III

What did Peter possess? Since he was unable to
give money to this beggar, what then was his contribution?

1. He gave him hope. There was little of high expectation in this beggar's heart before he met Peter.
The utmost for which he hoped was to be able to continue to beg enough to keep soul and body together

for a few more weary years. A beggar he was to-day,
a beggar he expected to remain to the end of the chapter. He had no thought of serving, no thought of
giving. He never dreamed of being a helper. The
weary road that stretched away before his feet was the
dull, drab, unromantic road of the parasite. But
Peter made him hope. Peter kindled in his heart the
expectation of the dawn of a better to-morrow.

It is a great privilege to be a hope bringer. There
are those in every congregation who seem especially
gifted of God for this high task. They know how to
make a sobbing heart sing. They know how to make
clouded skies bright. And we need such desperately,
for their opposites are always with us. I have known
those who were more skilled in going through your
pockets than the Artful Dodger. They could leave
you thoroughly discouraged after a five minutes' conversation. Sometimes to even meet them on the street
was to be depressed. But this man's expectation rose
from the dead in the presence of this apostle. Peter
gave him hope.

2. Peter gave him faith. He gave him faith in
man. This beggar came somehow to believe in Peter.
He was brought also to a new faith in himself. He
began to believe that he might be and do something
in the world. He was led to a new and uplifting
faith in Christ. Peter preached to him, and he
preached in such a fashion as to give him a daring
and vigorous faith.

3. Peter gave him love. Scores of people had put
money into the beggar's hands, but they had despised
him while they served him. They had scorned while
they helped him. He would have thrown their money
back into their faces but for the fact that hunger made

him refrain. He had possibly felt many times like
the beggar in Lowell's poem. The Knight threw him
a bit of gold, but there was no love in the gift. So:

> "The beggar left the coin in the dust.
> Better to me the poor man's crust
> Though he turn me empty from his door."

This beggar was sure of Peter's love. It was a love
that expressed itself. That is what love is always seeking to do. Peter stretched a helping hand to him:
"And he took him by the right hand and lifted him
up." He gave him the handclasp of a brother. It
seems a very simple gift, and yet there is none that is
more needed to-day and always.

IV

What was the outcome of Peter's giving?

1. This beggar was re-made. The man who had
never before stood upon his own feet was able to stand
erect. The man who was physically infirm became
physically strong. The man who was morally weak
became morally strong. So this apostle, in spite of
his empty pockets and his depleted bank account, was
still able to give gifts so rich and priceless that the one
privileged to receive them was utterly transformed.

2. Peter's gifts not only resulted in the re-making
of this beggar, but they passed on to the enriching
of other lives. When Peter reached the prayer meeting
that day, he brought somebody besides himself. There
was a man with him who had never been to prayer meeting before. He had been to the door, but he had never
managed to get in. There was a new face at the prayer

meeting. There was a new man, and he was not carried there. He went there "walking and leaping and praising God." And many at that prayer service were blessed by his presence. And I dare to believe that he will be a blessing to you and to me at this very service.

V

It is evident, therefore, that all God needs to bring about victory is for us to give what we have. It is true here, it is true everywhere. Here is a man named Moses. God wants to send him on a difficult mission. Moses is timid. He hesitates. "What is that in thy hand?" God asks. "It is a rod," is the answer. "Only a crooked stick." "Throw it down. Dedicate it to me," God says. Moses throws it down. It becomes a serpent. He picks it up again. It is a rod once more. It is the very same that it was before, with this difference. It is one that has been dedicated to God. Armed with this rod Moses invades the great Kingdom of Egypt and succeeds in the emancipation of his people.

There was a lad once who was used of Christ for the feeding of thousands of people. Yet this boy had only five loaves and two fish. How then was he able to accomplish such a great and impossible task? He did not do so by saying what he would do if he had a corner on the wheat market. He did not do so by eating the lunch that he had and saying how sorry he was that he did not have enough to feed the multitude. He accomplished this great task by simply giving Jesus what he had. He might have used the exact language of Peter—"What I have I give."

The most famous contribution of all history was

made by a certain poor widow. It was a contribution so large that it has made her immortal. We count her as one of heaven's multimillionaires. Many who were rich gave much that day, but this widow gave more than all. How came it that one so poor could give so much? Again, her secret is that of Peter. With only two mites in her hand she dared to approach her Lord and say, "What I have I give."

There is a certain character in the Bible to whom the world has given the name "Good." We can never forget this man. He is remembered not because he was the shrewd Samaritan or the brilliant Samaritan or the rich Samaritan. We remember him because he was the "Good Samaritan." And how did he earn this magnificent name? He did not do so by boasting of what he would do for a certain wounded man if he had only had medical training. We call him good because when he came face to face with a great need he gave what he had. He was not a physician, but he bound up a man's wounds the best he could. He had no ambulance, but he used a blundering donkey. He gave what he had and the wounded man was saved. He gave what he had and the world has crowned him. And better still, God has crowned him.

"What I have I give." If everybody would do that, the world would be won before sunset. And, mark you, it will never be won in any other way. God needs the gifts of the brilliant and talented. He needs the gifts of the man of genius. But just as genuinely does he need the gifts of those of us who are ordinary. God tunes the voice of the mocking bird to sing all the songs in the birds' hymn book. But He does not expect this mocker to be the only singer in His feathered choir.

He is quite as much interested in the songs of the least
gifted and the least tuneful. The world has been
greatly blessed by the gifts of the conspicuous workers.
But its greatest blessings have come through the faithful gifts of the hidden and the obscure.

I was on a battlefield some months ago. Here and
there I stopped before monuments to read the names
of those who "had paid the last sad measure of devotion." In the course of my ramble I came to a monument that bore no name. Inscribed upon it instead
were these words: "To the Unknown Dead." It was
erected in memory of those who gave their all, but forgot to sign their names. When the subscription list
was passed they made their offering. It was this:
"One life." And when we said: "Name, please," all
they answered was, "Never mind, write it down 'A
friend who loved the cause.'" They had no great gifts
of genius, but what they had they gave. They were so
busy giving in fact that they forgot to leave their
names.

> "Common as the wayside grasses,
>   Ordinary as the soil,
>   By the score he daily passes,
>   Going to and from his toil.
>   Stranger he to wealth and fame—
>   He is only What's-His-Name.
>
> "Cheerful 'neath the load he's bearing,
>   For he always bears a load;
>   Patiently forever faring
>   On his ordinary road;
>   All his days are much the same—
>   Uncomplaining What's-His-Name.

"Not for him is glittering glory,
Not for him the places high;
Week by week the same old story—
Try and fail and fail and try,
Life for him is dull and tame—
Poor, old, plodding What's-His-Name.

"Though to some one else the guerdon,
Though but few his worth may know;
On his shoulders rests the burden
Of our progress won so slow.
Red the road by which we came
With the blood of What's-His-Name."

Oh, my brethren, our task is simple. It is as simple as that at which Simon Peter worked. We are to be able to write our autobiographies with one sentence: "I give." If we can do that we write ourselves as kinsfolk to God Himself. The most blessed word we read about Him is this: "I give." And nothing better can we write or read about ourselves. Our task is giving, and what we are to give is not the wealth of another; we are to give what we have. Our pockets may be as empty as those of the apostle Peter, but that does not mean that we must be useless. We can still say: "Silver and gold have I none, but what I have I give."

XII

DOUBTING CASTLE—JOHN THE BAPTIST

Matthew 11: 3

"Art thou he that should come, or do we look
for another?"

This question was asked by John the Baptist. He
did not ask it in the atmosphere of the class room. He
did not ask it while he was enjoying the privilege of
his work in the out-of-doors. He did not ask it with
the applause of his cheering followers ringing in his
ears. He did not ask it amidst the luxuries of a palace.
He asked it while he was occupying a prison cell. He
asked it amidst the stenchful gloom of a dungeon
where the sunlight was a stranger, and where no physical comforts ever came.

I

Why did John ask this question?
He did not ask it for purposes of argument or specu-
lation. He did not ask it because he had become im-
patient with the slowness of Jesus and wanted to com-
pel Him to show His hand. He did not ask it to satisfy his own wavering disciples. He asked it to satisfy himself. John's faith has gone into eclipse.
There was a man preaching out in the open that he
had declared to be the promised Messiah. But now he

133

is in the grip of a chilling fear that he has made a mistake. His former certainty has given place to uncertainty. Therefore, he asks this question: "Art thou he that should come, or do we look for another?"

You remember in Bunyan's immortal allegory how his pilgrims wandered out of the way and went to sleep on strange soil. The next morning they were waked to find themselves in the grip of Giant Despair. This grim giant led them roughly away and thrust them into a dark and stenchful dungeon. The name of this fearful dungeon was "Doubting Castle." Now it was in this same dungeon that John the Baptist found himself. That was the reason he asked this question. And, mark you, he is not the only one of God's saints that has been imprisoned there. You have possibly passed not a few days of darkness and nights of wretchedness in this same grim castle. The floors of this gloomy prison are damp with the tears of some of the choicest sons and daughters of God. Its walls yet echo with the voice of their prayers. Elijah has been here. And so has Thomas. And so have countless others. It is a trying experience that few escape.

II

What was the cause of John's doubt?

His uncertainty did not grow out of the fact that he had never become acquainted with Jesus. That may be the secret of the doubt of some of us. Maybe you have never really met the Lord. Maybe you have never in true heart earnestness said to Him, "My Lord and my God." Maybe you have never been able to sing: "Blessed assurance, Jesus is mine." But this was not the case with John. He knew Jesus. John had baptised Him. He had been privileged to see the Spirit of God come in bodily form as a dove upon Him. And the message had already come to John that upon whom he should see the Spirit descending and remaining, the same was He that should baptise with the Holy Ghost. He had heard the voice of God saying: "This is my beloved Son, in whom I am well pleased."

Not only had John come to know Jesus for himself, but he had borne witness to Jesus. He had pointed his own disciples to Him. He had preached in one sentence a sermon that is the sum of all saving sermons: "Behold the Lamb of God which taketh away the sin of the world." John had seen in this man that he was now doubting the One of whom the Prophet spoke, "He was wounded for our transgressions, He was bruised for our iniquities: the chastisement of our peace was upon Him; and with His stripes we are healed. All we like sheep have gone astray; we have turned every one to his own way; and the Lord hath laid on Him the iniquity of us all." Therefore, John was not doubting for lack of personal knowledge of Jesus.

Neither was he doubting because he had fallen into sin. Sin is a most frequent cause of doubt. There is nothing that more surely saps our faith than conscious sin. You can sin against your deepest convictions till they cease to be convictions. You can outrage your conscience till it loses its voice of warning. The only way to continue to believe your beliefs is by putting them into practice. But John had put his into practice. It would be hard to find one who had done so more courageously.

Look at this picture. John has begun preaching in the wilderness. So arresting is his message, so com-

pelling is his earnest personality that he empties the
cities round about and crowds the wilderness with the
eager throngs. He speaks fearlessly to the hearts and
consciences of men. He urges upon them the necessity
of repentance. And men of all classes are moved by
him. Men of all classes accept his baptism. Therefore, his fame so spreads that he is invited to preach
at the court of Herod.

Here he is put to a very sharp test. It is evident
that Herod admires him. He is much impressed by
him. But he rebukes Herod's sin. He does not tell
him that it is not expedient for him to live the corrupt
life he is living. He tells him that it is not lawful.
He makes him smart. He makes him tremble. For
this courageous stand Herod's harlot has John put in
prison. But he goes to his prison cell with the consciousness that he has done his duty as God has given
him to see his duty. So John's doubt was not born of
his unfaithfulness.

1. John was idle. Idleness is exceedingly hard to
endure. A graduate of Princeton University wrote
some time ago: "I am dying of nothing to do." His
father had left him a fortune. Work was unnecessary.
Since work was unnecessary, he refused to work.
Therefore, he found himself dying by the inch. Unable to endure the torture, he put a pistol to his temple and blew his brains out. He might have saved himself by going to work, but he preferred the easier path
of suicide.

Multitudes die from the same cause in the Church
every year. For, mark you, no man is strong enough
to be a Christian and be deliberately idle. Such a
thing is an utter impossibility. This is true, because
idleness is in itself a sin. "To him that knoweth to do

good and doeth it not, to him it is sin." Then idleness persisted in leads inevitably to positive sin. Nature abhors a vacuum. If a man will not fill his hands with positive good, then sooner or later he will fill them with positive evil. There is only one sure method of victory over sin and that is to roll against it an overcoming tide of good.

But John was not willingly idle. He was idle because he could not help himself. His idleness was enforced. Yet even this form of idleness is hard to endure. That is the reason that knights of the sick room find it very hard to keep a sunny and vigorous faith. That is the reason that old bodies who are no longer able to work find it so easy to look backward to a golden age instead of forward. The good days were the days when they were on the firing line. Now the grace of God is sufficient to keep one sunny even in the midst of enforced idleness, but much grace is needed. John did not avail himself of that needed grace. Hence his faith went into eclipse.

2. John misunderstood Jesus.

(1) John was perplexed by the work Jesus was doing in the world. He had expected the Messiah to perform tasks that were altogether different from the ones that Jesus was performing. The Christ that he had preached was one who had a fan in His hand. He was to thoroughly cleanse the threshing floors. The wheat He was to gather into garners and the chaff He was to burn with unquenchable fire. Every tree that did not bear good fruit He was to cut down. He was to rescue His oppressed people and enable them to put their feet upon the neck of their oppressor.

His conception of Christ's work, therefore, was physical rather than spiritual. He thought the Kingdom of God was to come with observation. He believed that Christ's conquests were to be outward and political rather than inward and moral. He looked for a victory such as only physical weapons could achieve. His expectations did not rise to the height of those who realise that the supreme victory is that wrought by those weapons that are not carnal.

There are those to-day who are depressed and discouraged and in doubt for this same reason. Such people often claim that Christianity has failed. But in making such complaint they indicate their failure to realise Christ's method of work and also His purpose in the world. Christ is not here to win a victory through physical force. He is here to make the appeal of love to the hearts of men. If men yield to that appeal, He wins. If they refuse that appeal, He loses so far as they are concerned. Christ's Kingdom cannot come only in but one way, and that is through the yielding of our hearts to the appeal of the divine love.

(2) Then John was perplexed by the dealing of Christ with himself. John was suffering. Not only so, but he was suffering unjustly. If he had been unfaithful to Jesus, it would have been far easier for him to have understood the hard ordeal through which he was passing. But he had not been unfaithful. He had not played the coward. He had not shirked. He had not turned his back upon his Master. He had marched breast forward. He had been unflinchingly loyal when loyalty cost him everything.

Now the One to whom he had been loyal was at liberty in the big outer world. He was out there preaching to the poor. He was opening blind eyes. He was cleansing lepers. He was even raising the dead. Evidently He had power. He had power beyond the human. Why then did He not exercise that power in his own behalf? Why did He not pay him for his loyalty and for his faithfulness by breaking down his prison door and working for his physical deliverance? Many have been perplexed by this same problem. Men have somehow felt all through the centuries that God ought to pay them wages for being loyal. But this is not His method. The Devil pays wages. God never does. "The wages of sin is death, but the gift of God is eternal life, through Jesus Christ, our Lord."

Some weeks ago I received a letter that read a bit like this: "A little more than a year ago my business partner left me and went into the bootlegging business. He urged me to join him, but I refused because I could not get the consent of my conscience to engage in such an evil enterprise. He laughed at my scruples and went his way. Since then I have not prospered. But my friend has grown rich. He lives now on Massachusetts Avenue. He has two or three high-powered cars and plenty of servants. What I want to know is if it pays to do right?"

And what could I answer this man? What would you have answered? There was but one answer to give and that was a very definite affirmative. Certainly it pays to do right. Certainly it pays to be loyal to God and to your conscience. That does not mean, however, that it pays in dollars and cents. There is no place in the Bible where you are promised so much per day for being a saint. Other things being equal, the genuine Christian has the better chance at material prosperity. But when he does prosper, his prosperity is a by-product. God does not promise financial or political or social success to any man for being righteous. Christ is not in the world primarily to make men successful. He is not here to make men rich. He is not here to give men an easy time. He is not here chiefly to exempt men from pain and from hardship and from conflict and from struggle. He is here that we might have life, and that we might have it in abundance. And He spares no pains on the part of Himself or of ourselves in order to reach this end.

For this reason all prison doors are not opened, even for God's saints. For this reason all fiery furnaces are not abolished. For this reason all tears are not dried. There are pains that come to us that we must endure to the end. There are thorns that pierce us that must continue to pierce us till the very last hour of the twilight. There are agonies that torture us that will keep up their torture even till the coming of night. This is true not because our Lord does not love us. It is true because He does love us. He loves us so well that He is willing to allow us to suffer in order to bring us to a fuller and larger life. John did not realise this. Therefore, his own personal agony made him doubt.

III

What did John do with his doubt?

1. He defied it. He did not allow it to turn his feet from the plain path of duty. He did not allow it to swerve him an inch from the road of righteousness. Frederick W. Robertson was like him in this respect. He, too, was tortured by doubt. But through it all, with the realisation that right is ever right, he clung to the right as God had given him to see it. He lived up to the truth insofar as it was revealed.

Hear again this question: "Art thou He that should come, or do we look for another?" "It may be," says John, "that I have been deceived. It may be that thou art not the Coming One. Even if I have been mistaken, of this I am sure, that God is going to make good His promise. If thou art not the Coming One, then there is another. Therefore, I will not turn my back toward the eastern horizon. I will face the East in the expectation that the Sun of Righteousness will yet rise with healing in his beams. I will mount my watchtower and keep a constant lookout till the promised Messiah does come."

2. John carried his doubt to Jesus. He did not consult the enemies of Jesus as some do. He went to Jesus Himself. And, mark you, that is every man's privilege. We do not need any go-between here. We do not need a priest. We do not need the Virgin Mary. We do not need the saints. We have, every one of us, the privilege of a personal appeal to Jesus Christ Himself.

And what said Jesus thus appealed to? Did He reply that He had no patience with a doubter? Did He show any anger at Nathanael as he doubted if any good thing could come out of Nazareth? Was He angry with Peter when he sank under the weight of his doubts? Was He angry with the two disciples who walked that Easter Sunday from Jerusalem to Emmaus? Was He angry with Thomas when Thomas so brutally said that he would not believe unless he put his fingers in the print of the nails and thrust his hand into His side?

No, He was not angry. When they came to Him in sincerity wanting to know He replied to them. He gave them certainty for uncertainty. He gave them faith instead of fear. And so He replied to John. He said to the two who interviewed Him on behalf of their master: "Go tell John the things that you see and hear; how that the lepers are cleansed and the lame walk and the blind receive their sight and the dead are raised up and the poor have the Gospel preached to them." And though we are not told what John said when these messengers returned, yet I have a conviction that he was entirely satisfied.

And to you who are troubled and perplexed, I bring this message: Jesus Christ is able to meet your need. He is able to dispel your doubts. He is able to bring you into a place of blessed certainty. His grace is sufficient for you. Appeal to Him. "Come boldly unto the throne of grace." Do this and you will go away from His house to-day with the conviction that He satisfies the longing soul. You will go away singing: "I will bless the Lord at all times. His praise shall continually be in my month. For I sought the Lord and He heard me and delivered me from all my fears."

He will also deliver u if u give them a chance

XIII

LOVE IS DEAD—THE LEPER

Mark 1:40

"If thou wilt, thou canst make me clean."

I

This is a very pathetic prayer. It is deeply marked with heartache, disillusionment and bitter disappointment. It is soaked in despairful tears. "If thou wilt, thou canst make me clean." "I believe that thou hast the power, but I hardly think that thou wouldst care to exercise it in my behalf. Thou hast the necessary ability, but I am in doubt about thy love." "If thou wilt, thou canst make me clean."

What is the matter with this poor fellow? He has lost faith in love. He still believes in power, but for him love is dead. There have been glad days in his past, doubtless, when he believed in love. There were yesterdays that were tender and bright and beautiful because the light of love illuminated them. But they have all dropped into the sunset. Black night is upon him now because he believes that love is dead.

II

It is easy to imagine how he came into this sad state. He was not a deliberate cynic. He had not made up his mind to believe in the complete selfishness of every one in an effort to excuse his own selfishness. There are those who are guilty of such conduct, you know. But such was not the case with this man. He had come to this sad state because of his terrible suffering. His faith in the fact of love had been pounded out of him by hard-fisted pain. He had suffered long and alone and hopelessly.

1. He was a victim of physical disease. He was a leper. He had a malady that was most loathsome and horrible. It was a disease that made him ghastly in the eyes of every beholder. It was a dogged sickness that was eating him up piecemeal. The man who died of it had to see himself drop into his grave by the inch. Suffering thus, it is not to be wondered at that, if he had had no other pain, he lived in the torture of a perpetual nightmare.

2. He was unfriended and alone. His physical suffering was the least of his agonies. When his leprosy stole upon him, more fearful than the ghastly death that he saw in the distance was the thought of separation from all that he loved. For his malady made its victim unclean. It drove him from the fellowship of his kind. It scourged him from the haunts of men. His lips might ache for the kiss of wife and child, but they must ache in vain. And the home to which he was sent was not one where every comfort was provided. It was a cave or an open grave. To such an abode this man had gone. Here he had lived unvisited and uncared for till he felt himself utterly forgotten. Here he had suffered, despised, neglected and alone.

3. He was seemingly forsaken of the Lord. Not only had he been separated from his fellows, but he felt himself utterly separated from God. He had been

taught to believe that the fact that this ghastly disease
had come upon him was a mark of the Divine dis-
pleasure. The fact that he had thus suffered showed
that he was under the frown of God. That is why he
had been thrown out among the filth and rubbish of the
tombs. He was a creature so inwardly and outwardly
rotten as to be unfit for the fellowship either of God or
of man. Naturally he had come under such suffering
to be sceptical about the very existence of love. He did
not believe there was a man on earth or a God in
heaven who really cared for him.

III

But one day strange rumours came to him. Most
amazing stories were told about a young Rabbi who
was doing works out in the big world that were beyond
the human. Some had declared that he had healed
the sick, that he had shown skill to open the eyes of
the blind and let the morning in. In these stories he
at first took only mild interest. They did not concern
him personally in the least. Why should they? He
was as one already dead. He was no longer a part of
that world of which these stories were told. That
world had forgotten him, had broken his heart and
thrown him utterly away.

Then one day a traveller passed his way whose step
was made quick by irrepressible joy. His face was
wonderfully sunny, and he seemed bent on telling his
story to any one who was willing to listen. And when
this leper cried, "Unclean! unclean!" at his approach,
he did not flee away. On the contrary, he came close
enough to speak to him. And a wonderful story he
had to tell! "Yesterday I was blind," he cries joy-

fully, "but I met Jesus of Nazareth and He cured me. You just ought to go to Him. He can cure any disease."

And there was such a ring of sincerity in the testimony that the leper found it impossible to doubt. "I think this physician could cure me," he said to himself, "if he only cared to do so. I believe that he is able to cure me, and maybe he would want to do so if he only knew how wretched I am. Maybe he could be led to care if he could only see how this awful leprosy is gnawing the flesh from my body. Oh, if he knew how long are my nights; if he knew how bitter are my days; if he knew how dead weary I become of this long fisticuff with death, surely he would help me. I believe I will try him. Anything is better than sitting here and seeing yourself slip into the grave by the inch."

Thus this unhappy wretch decides that he will at least make an effort. He makes up his mind to do something. Others may stay in their tombs and wish they were sound and well, but he knows that wishing will not get him anywhere. It is well to wish that you were a better man; it is well to wish that you were clean, but all that comes to naked nothing unless you act. It is not enough to sit idle and wish. You have got to do something. This man decided that he would not let this only chance of salvation pass by while he sat in idleness. If he had to die, he would at least die after giving himself this one possible chance.

So he came to Jesus. I know he came without a full orbed faith. He was beset by many a doubt. He was exceedingly uncertain of his reception. He was hampered by his disease. He was hampered by his fear of the crowd. He knew that the people about

Jesus would not welcome him. He was dogged and
hounded by a hundred fears. But in spite of his
meagre faith and in spite of all his difficulties, he did
come. And that, mark you, is more than many of us
have done. We have heard the Gospel from our infancy. The Bible has been an open book in our homes.
We have heard sermons enough to save the world. We
have looked wistfully toward the heights and have at
times longed to be better. But in spite of our chances,
we have never yet come to Jesus. In spite of all our
good impulses, we have never come to fling ourselves
down at His feet. This man came to Jesus.

IV

Not only did he come, but he prayed. Listen again
to his pathetic plea! "Lord, if thou wilt, thou canst
make me clean." It is a very humble prayer. The
story says that he threw himself down at the feet of
Jesus. People can pray standing; they can pray in
any position in the world, and they can take the most
humble attitudes, and yet fail to pray. But I somehow
feel that the kneeling position is the most natural, especially when we are really humble in our hearts.
When you get heart hungry, when you feel that your
situation is desperate, when you feel that your need
is compelling beyond all words, it becomes quite natural for you to get down on your knees. The leper was
humble in his attitude. He was so because he was
truly humble in his heart.

Listen to him! He makes no claim for himself
whatsoever. He comes with no parading of any fancied soundness there might be in him. He tells the
Lord frankly that he is unclean. When he said, "Thou

canst make me clean," that was a confession that he was not clean. And that was the first step also toward getting clean. If you are all that you ought to be, then you have no need of Jesus. If you are white and unspotted, then there is no place for you at the foot of the cross. "They that are whole need not a physician, but they that are sick." It was to seek and to save those that are lost that Jesus came. If you are not ready to confess your sin, then you are not ready to find salvation.

This man has no plea to make except the plea of his own deep need. "Thou canst make me clean." That is a confession that the task is beyond himself. He cannot cure himself; he is wise enough to know that. So are you, if you are a man of any moral earnestness at all. If you have ever made any serious effort to live right, you have at least come to this discovery: that you are powerless to resist evil in your own strength. No man is in himself equal to the task of conquering sin in his own life. Every man who with any degree of earnestness undertakes it must come at last to that heart-breaking cry of St. Paul, "Oh, wretched man that I am, who shall deliver me." This man knows that he needs help. "Lord, I am unclean. Lord, I must remain unclean to the end of eternity except I am cleansed by thee. I cannot cleanse myself. Man cannot cleanse me. 'Not all Neptune's ocean can sweeten' this rotting body. There is no chance for me except at thy hands. 'And now, Lord, what wait I for, my hope is in thee. If thou wilt, thou canst make me clean.'"

You can see that this leper believed in the power of Christ. He believed in His might. He was sure that Jesus was able to cure him, even if he was not sure of

His willingness. Have you got that far along, you who were cradled in the arms of a Christian mother? Do you believe that the Son of God is able to make you absolutely free? Or have you let the Devil convince you that it is impossible for you to ever be delivered from sin? Are you yielding complacently to-day to your own selfishness, to your own lust, to your own evil habits because you have concluded that you can do nothing else? Do you believe that there is a sin from which Christ cannot save you, or do you believe what the word teaches: "He is able to save unto the uttermost them that come unto God by Him"? This man believed in the power of Christ.

But here his faith broke down. Though he believed in the power of Christ, he doubted His love. "If thou wilt, thou canst." It is as if he said: "Jesus, Master, I am not sure that you will care to heal me. I fear it does not matter to you whether I go or come, rise or sink, live and laugh and love, or suffer and sob and rot. I am certain of your power, but I am uncertain of your love."

V

Now, do not be too hard on this man. It is not always easy for us to-day with all our light to believe in the love of God. It is no trouble to believe in His power. We see evidence of that everywhere. We read of His might in the majesty of the templed hills, in the rugged mountain heights, in the vast ocean and in the shimmering stars. It is not hard to believe that our God is a mighty God. But when we turn to these same things for the tokens of His love, we do not always find them. The mountain hurls her stones and her avalanches to the destruction of human life. The tempests swoop down upon the defenceless and they are swept away. The ocean shakes itself in its rage and swallows the crippled ship as ruthlessly as any sea monster. Wherein do we find the proof of the love of God? The mountains say: "It is not in us." The skies say: "It is not in us." Nowhere, in fact, in nature do we find sure proof of the healing, cleansing, forgiving love of God.

So we find it hard at times to believe in the love of God. And yet how much better chance we have than this man had. He did not know that the man who stood before him was going to the cross for him in a few more months. He did not know that that brow bent above him was soon to be crowned with thorns for his sake. He had never heard that message pulsating with deathless hopes for the last and the lowest and the least of us: "For God so loved the world that He gave His only begotten Son, that whosoever believeth in Him should not perish but have everlasting life." This fact is most familiar to us. And yet, even we at times doubt the love of God. Therefore, it is not to be wondered at that this battered and tossed and bruised piece of human wreckage did not find it easy to believe in Christ's love for him.

But if there was some doubt in his prayer, it was deeply honest and genuinely sincere. He did not claim a faith that he did not possess. He did not come with an avowal of trust upon his lips when utter doubt was in his heart. He was downright honest and frank in that pathetic prayer of his. And it is my conviction that our prayer life would be enriched greatly if we would cultivate the habit of absolute sincerity in dealing with Christ. "He looketh on the heart," remem-

ber. There is no use in claiming a faith that we do
not possess. There is no use in professing submission
when our hearts are in hot rebellion. Let us dare to be
honest with Him and frank with Him, as was this man,
who told Him just what was in his heart.

VI

And what was the result?

1. Christ had compassion on him. He did not repel
him. He did not drive him away because he did not
have a perfectly well-rounded faith. He did not and
never does. He ever makes good the promise, "Him
that cometh unto me I will in no wise cast out." This
man came blunderingly, hampered with doubt. But
this big, blessed fact remains: He did come. And
when he prayed his humble, sincere prayer, "If thou
wilt, thou canst make me clean," Jesus did not repel
him. He had compassion on him."

Notice the word. "He had compassion on him." It
is something finer than pity. You can pity people
without loving them, but you cannot have compassion
unless there is love in your heart. "He had compassion on him." He entered into sympathy with him.
He got down under his load with him. He smarted
through his wounds and suffered in his broken heart
and wept through his tears. "He had compassion on
him."

2. Christ touched him. That was the outcome of
his compassion. Compassion is an active something.
You can pity folks and do nothing. It is altogether
possible that the priest and the Levite pitied that poor,
wounded fellow whom they found dying by the road-
side, but the Good Samaritan had compassion on him.

And, having compassion, he went to him and bound up his wounds and took him to an inn and took care of him. Christ had compassion on this leper, and, having compassion, He touched him.

That touch was the spontaneous act of love. The leper recognised that fact instantly. He no longer doubted love, no longer thought love dead. He knew it was alive and active. Love was putting its helping hand upon him. It was touching him. And it was this touch that woke up the dead love in his own heart. When Jesus put his hands upon him, his own dead love stirred, opened its eyes and smiled, and came into vigorous and joyous life.

3. Christ healed him. It was no trouble now for this leper to believe that Jesus cared. The touch convinced him. There was nothing in the world of which he was so sure. Such a touch always makes us sure. It is an indication that the one who so touches has identified himself with us, is getting under our load. It brings conviction that he is going to help us so far as is in his power, because he loves us. It was that touch that made it possible for Jesus to cure this leper. I do not believe the cure would have been possible without it, because the leper would not have sufficiently believed in Jesus to open his heart to Him.

And there is no exception to the rule. When Jesus wanted to save the world, there was no cheaper way for Him to do so than by identifying Himself with that world. "Forasmuch then as the children are partakers of flesh and blood He also Himself took part of the same." Before Jesus could save us and lift us out of our ruin utter and complete back again to God, He must needs bridge the wide chasm that separates man

and God and identify Himself with us. And there is
no cheaper method for you and me. We must identify
ourselves with those whom we would help.

Years ago a young man offered himself for membership in a certain church. The preacher asked him
about his conversion, and he said he owed his conversion
to Henry Drummond. The preacher next asked him
what Mr. Drummond said to him. "He said nothing,"
was the reply, "he simply put his hand on my shoulder
and looked at me." But there was that in the touch
that broke his heart and brought him to Christ, because
it was a touch of real sympathy born of real love. It
was a brother's touch. And there is nothing that this
old world needs to-day so much as the touch of a
brother. It will be saved, it will be won to Christ, it
will be softened and mellowed and wooed in no other
way.

"When a man ain't got a cent
        And is feelin' kinder blue,
And the clouds hang low and heavy,
        And won't let the sunshine through,
It is a great thing, O my brethren,
        For a fellow just to lay
His hand upon your shoulder
        In a friendly sort o' way.

"It makes a man feel curious,
        And it makes the teardrops start,
And you sorter feel a flutter
        In the region of the heart,
And you can't look up and meet his eye,
        And you don't know what to say,
When his hand is on your shoulder
        In a friendly sort o' way.

"Oh, the world's a curious compound,
　With its honey and its gall,
　With its cares and bitter crosses,
　But a good world after all;
　And a good God must have made it,
　Leastwise that is what I say
　When his hand is on my shoulder
　In a friendly sort o' way."

4. Christ cured him immediately. "Jesus stretched
forth His hand and touched him and said, I will, be
thou clean. And as soon as He had spoken, immediately the leprosy departed from him and he was
cleansed." "I am willing," said Jesus, and the man
was cured. He was cured at once. He did not have
to wait. He did not have to go mourning for days and
weeks and months and years. He was cured immediately. Thank God for immediate salvation. Thank
God for One who is able instantly to loose us from our
sins and wash us and make us whiter than snow. I
preach to you to-night on immediate salvation. This
salvation you may have now, at this very moment, this
very instant. You do not have to even wait until the
sermon is ended. You can be saved by the power of
God right now.

"I am willing," said Jesus to this man who was uncertain about His willingness. He had been willing all
along to cure him and make him whole, but the trouble
was that the man was not willing. Do you think that
the Lord is willing to save you? Do you think that
the reason that you are away from Christ to-night is
that He does not want you? Is your Godlessness due
to the unwillingness of Christ to save you, or to your
own unwillingness to be saved? Oh, you know where
the fault is. It is not with Him, it is with you.

Yonder stands Jesus sobbing over the city that He loved. "How often," He said, "would I have gathered thy children as a hen gathers her brood under her wing, and ye would not." That is, "I was willing to save, I was willing to shelter you, I was willing to give you a place in my loving care, but you did not want it." And God cannot save any man against his will. But the fact that Jerusalem was lost, and the fact that any man is lost, is not the fault of the unwillingness of Christ, but of the unwillingness of the one who refuses His salvation.

Will you be saved to-night? Jesus is willing. He is willing to work an immediate deliverance. He is willing to receive you and make you every whit whole. But His willingness will go for nothing, His love will go for nothing, His cross will go for nothing so far as you are concerned, unless you are willing. It all hinges there. It is a question of your own willingness and of that only. He has declared His willingness times innumerable. He has declared it in the pathetic language of the cross. And now He waits for you. Believe me, there is nothing that will keep you from His cleansing except your own unwillingness to come and be cleansed. Will you let Him speak this word to your heart? "I will. Be thou clean."

XIV

A BEAUTIFUL WORK—MARY OF BETHANY

Mark 14:6

"She hath wrought a beautiful work on me."

I

This was the verdict of Jesus. Judas did not agree with Him. He had not the slightest admiration for Mary's deed. He did not think that it was beautiful in the least. He rather regarded it as an ugly bit of extravagance. He looked upon it as a foolish piece of waste. To him it was so much money absolutely thrown away. It was the sum of three hundred pence squandered for naked nothing. Judas felt somewhat as if Mary had taken this sum out of his own pocket. Therefore, her deed did not excite his admiration.

But Christ said that it was beautiful. Of course we accept the verdict of Jesus rather than the verdict of Judas.

1. We accept the verdict of Jesus because Jesus has the seeing eye. He sees things clearly and sees them whole. Judas, on the other hand, looked on everything with warped vision. His selfishness had poisoned his sight. He was not possessed of the single eye. Therefore, the very light that was within him was darkness. But Jesus had the single eye of love. Therefore, we know that a work that He calls beautiful is beautiful indeed.

156

2. We feel safe also in accepting this verdict of Jesus because He has lived from eternity to eternity in the realm of perfect beauty. There is no ugliness where He abides. Every face is winsome. Every soul is transfigured. Every song is perfect in its melody. Every flower is fair and unfading. No landscape is marred. In this abode of perfect beauty Christ has lived from everlasting. Therefore, He is naturally skilled in His judgment of what is beautiful.

3. We may accept the verdict of Jesus because He is the creator of beauty. There is nothing beautiful in heaven or on earth that was not fashioned by His fingers. His might kindled every sun. He gave the gleam to every star. He clothes the lily with a glory surpassing that of Solomon. He paints the wing of the butterfly. He crimsons the East with dawn. He makes the death of the day as winsome as its birth by the glory of His sunsets. Therefore, since He is the creator of all that is beautiful, He can speak with authority on the subject of beauty.

II

What was there beautiful about this deed?

1. It was beautiful in its motive. When Mary anointed her Lord she was not simply seeking a place in the limelight. She was not selfishly struggling to have herself remembered. She was not trying to win the applause of the crowd. What she did was done because of her keen devotion to her Lord. This work that she wrought was born of the highest possible motive, the motive of love to Jesus Christ Himself.

Now it is almost trite to say that no deed can ever be beautiful that is born of a mean and ignoble and selfish motive. The music that selfishness makes is only "a sounding brass and a clanging cymbal." The flowers that selfishness sends are only nettles and nightshade and obnoxious weeds. The jewels that selfishness gives are only so much paltry glass. Every deed, however seemingly fair it may be, becomes unsightly and ugly when we realise that it was born of a mean and impure motive.

Take the kiss of Judas, for instance. Suppose Judas had kissed Jesus because he loved Him. Suppose he had kissed Him in token of the fact that he was determined to be loyal to Him. Suppose that when the soldiers and the mob came to arrest Jesus, Judas had stepped bravely forward and had said: "Jesus, Master, the world may forsake you, the world may turn against you and crucify you, but I want you to know that you have my loyalty and my love now and evermore. And in token of my devotion to you, I bestow upon you this kiss." Had Judas' motive been pure, he would have been regarded as about the sweetest saint of sacred story. But as it is he is the most hated. This is the case not because the deed he did was ugly in itself. It is true because it was done from an ugly motive.

Now, while no gift is truly beautiful that is done through a wrong motive, it is equally true that the very smallest deed becomes beautiful when it is done from a noble motive. Some months ago I sat talking to a mother. Suddenly a little laddie of about three summers came upon the scene and broke into the conversation. He had been out playing in the yard. His little apron was soiled and his face was soiled. His fist was also soiled. But he held that little dirty fist up to his mother and said: "Mother, I brought you a bouquet." I could not see any bouquet, but when he opened his hand there lay in his palm one little withered dog fennel blossom.

Could any gift. be smaller or meaner than that? Who wants a dog fennel blossom? How natural it would have been for this mother to have pushed the little fellow aside and said: "Take that ugly thing and throw it out the window." But the mother did not look at the flower. She looked at the motive. Therefore, she gathered the little lad in her arms, kissed his face and kissed his soiled hand. As she kissed him this dog fennel blossom bloomed into a Marshal Neil rose. Yea, it became a veritable flower garden under the transfiguring power of love.

2. This deed was beautiful in its recklessness. There was a mad abandon about it. Mary might have anointed Jesus with a mere fraction of what was in that alabaster box. But with a lack of prudence and business sagacity, that was absolutely insane in the eyes of Judas, she lavished the whole of it upon her Lord. And Christ praised her for so doing. He was ever ready to eulogise the reckless giver, but never did He have a word of praise for the prudent and careful giver who was constantly counting the cost. This deed was beautiful in its lovely recklessness.

3. This deed was beautiful in its uniqueness. It was so thoroughly original. It was so winsomely individual. Mary could not make the contribution to this feast that her sister Martha made. Martha served. She waited on the table. She was good at that. But Mary was not. Her hands seemed to have no skill for such tasks. But because she could not make Martha's contribution, she did not refuse to make any at all.

Mary was a lover, you remember. And love is always eager to give. Since love is eager, it is inventive. It may do the conventional thing. It may do the ordinary and commonplace thing. But of this you may be sure, it will do something. It will find some mode of expression. You can no more hide love in the heart of an individual and expect that individual to stay still than you can hide springtime away in a garden and expect that garden not to express itself in terms of colour and perfume. Mary could not do what Martha could. Therefore, she did the beautifully unique deed that was within her reach.

4. This deed was beautiful in its timeliness. Many a work that would have been beautiful has lost all its beauty by being wrought too late. Many a gift that would have been worthful has lost most of its worth by being behind time. For instance, Nicodemus gave Jesus one hundred pounds of myrrh and aloes. But Jesus was dead then. This disciple, like many another, was too late.

But Mary was on time. "She came," Jesus says, "aforetime." With the fine intuition of love she looked down the way and saw death coming to her Lord, and she said: "I will beat death to Him." And so she did. She anointed Him while He was yet alive. And when death came and touched His brow, her deed made even death's frozen fingers to smell of perfume.

A few years ago I went to take an offering of flowers to a faded old grandmother. She was past eighty years of age. But she had told me weeks before about her birthday. And so I went in remembrance of that event and carried her a small offering of flowers. And her old face lighted up as she received the gift as it might have lighted if she had been sixteen and I had been her lover. And she smiled upon me through tears that she took no pains to conceal, and this is what she said: "Oh, I am so glad that you did not wait till I was dead to bring them." Mary's deed was beautiful in its timeliness.

III

What was the outcome of this beautiful work.

1. Incidentally this deed made the name of Mary immortal. Not that she was seeking this immortality. Had she performed this deed in order to be remembered, she would have doubtless been forgotten. The world is not diligent in preserving the names of those who are merely hungry for the limelight. This boon of an abiding place in the memory of Christ and of man came to her as a kind of by-product of her deed of devotion. She was not seeking to be remembered any more than we are to seek for that end for ourselves. She was seeking to serve, and in so seeking she won everlasting fame.

Now to be remembered is no mean privilege. None of us desires to be forgotten.

"Who to dumb forgetfulness a prey,
This pleasing, anxious being ere resigned,
Left the warm precincts of a cheerful day,
Nor cast one longing, lingering look behind."

Those of you who have visited South Cheyenne Canyon in Colorado will doubtless remember seeing a loose heap of stones upon a mountain top overlooking this lovely canyon. This is the spot where Helen Hunt Jackson was first buried. Her body has since been removed. She left this request to those who should visit the spot: They were to lay two stones upon her grave and take one away with them. Thus she sought to build an ever-growing monument. Thus she sought to keep alive her memory.

Now there was possibly much of mere selfish ambition in this. But we shrink from being forgotten even when we are utterly unselfish. One of the last words that our Lord left us is "Do this in remembrance of me." He yearns to be remembered. He does this not because he is vain and ambitious, but because He is unselfish and loving. There is no greater pain that can come to loving hearts than the pain of being forgotten by those that they love. Every lover is eager for an abiding place in the memory and the heart of the beloved.

For this reason it must have brought much joy to the heart of Mary when her Master told her that she should never be forgotten. Of course He himself remembered her. He remembered her during those tragic and trying last days. He remembered her amidst the betrayal of Judas and the denial of Peter. I think He remembered her, and strengthened His heart by that memory, amidst the conflict of Gethsemane and the agony of Calvary. And He remembers her still, now that He is seated at the right hand of the throne of the Majesty on high.

Not only does Christ remember her, but He sees to it that we do not forget. He has linked her name to His own by chains that cannot be broken. "Wheresoever this Gospel shall be preached throughout the whole world, this also that this woman has done shall be spoken of as a memorial of her." The memory of Mary of Bethany will last as long as the Gospel lasts. When the world has forgotten her, then it will have forgotten the story of Him who "was wounded for our transgressions and bruised for our iniquities."

2. This deed that Mary did helped Jesus. It warmed His heart. It served to strengthen Him for the terrible ordeal that was ahead of Him. I am aware of the fact that Judas said that the ointment was wasted. But Judas was mistaken. The trouble with Judas is that he did not have any scales that were capable of weighing such precious jewels as this. His scales might serve to weigh pig iron and fertiliser. They might serve very well the purposes of a junk dealer. But in the shop of one who deals in rare and priceless gems they would be entirely out of place. For nothing was of value to Judas unless it could be used to put bread into somebody's mouth or garments upon his body. He had absolutely no conception of a value that was not reckoned in terms of the material.

But we all know that there are many things that seem useless to men of the type of Judas that are exceedingly useful. There are many things that seem to such men unpractical that are after all exceedingly practical. What, for instance, is the value of a handshake? Ask Judas and he will tell you that it is worth absolutely nothing. It is so much wasted energy. And yet we know that there are times when such a seemingly useless something is worth far more than gold. Certainly that is the opinion of the man who, upon being asked how he was rescued from the slavery of drink, replied: "I was rescued through the handclasp of a friend."

What is the value of a smile? Here again the verdict of Judas would not be trustworthy. Judas might stop to salvage a wrecked piece of machinery, but he would throw such priceless things as smiles upon the scrap pile. But here again he would show his blindness. God has used as simple a thing as a smile to make a hopeless heart sing. He has used a smile for the re-making of a shattered and broken life. Therefore, there are times when smiles are of more value than precious jewels.

What is the good of a mother's kiss? Is there any healing power in it? Ask Judas and he will answer with an emphatic "No." He may tell you that kissing spreads disease. He will certainly assert that it has no power to heal our hurts. But those of us who remember our mothers know better. Just the other day a little fellow that belonged to a home where I was visiting fell and hurt himself. With face wet with tears, he hastened to his mother. This mother gathered him into her arms and said: "Yes, yes, tell mother where you are hurt." And the little fellow touched the bruised place upon his forehead. Then the mother kissed that place, and what do you suppose happened? The child's tears were dried, the pain was healed, and he went gladly again about his play.

We are not, therefore, to be taken in by the plausible criticism of Judas. "Why was this waste of the ointment made?" he questions. It might have been sold for three hundred pence and given to the poor. How businesslike that sounds! A very practical man is Judas, so he himself thought. So also thought his fellow disciples. For they agreed with him, you remember. But there are practical ways of helping that appeal neither to the palate nor to any other bodily comfort. There is a way to help that appeals to the heart. That was the way that Mary chose. And I dare to believe that in doing this deed that looked so utterly worthless in the eyes of Judas she rendered to Jesus the most helpful service that she could possibly have rendered.

3. This beautiful deed helped others. John tells us that the house was filled with the odour of the ointment. But it was impossible to confine this sweet fragrance within the narrow bounds of that one house. It floated out through the windows and spread and spread until it has gone literally round the world. It has been wafted across all oceans and into all lands. This sweet perfume is with us this morning as we worship together in the peace of God's house. Even now, though separated from this scene by seas and continents and centuries, our atmosphere is a bit sweeter because of Mary's winsome deed.

Now, what is the message that the fragrance of this deed brings to us to-day? It tells us that we may serve as Mary served. What did Mary? She did her best. She gave her all to Christ for love's sake. Our Master said of her, "She hath done what she could." That much you can do. That much I can do. And that is enough. If we do this, then one day we shall be privileged to share the reward of her of whom the Master said: "She hath wrought a beautiful work on me."

XV

THE DRUDGE—THE ELDER SON

Luke 15 : 25-32

"Now his elder son was in the field: and as he came and drew nigh to the house, he heard music and dancing. And he called one of the servants and asked what these things meant. And he said unto him, Thy brother is come; and thy father hath killed the fatted calf, because he hath received him safe and sound. And he was angry, and would not go in; therefore came his father out and entreated him. And he answering said to his father, Lo, these many years do I serve thee, neither transgressed I at any time thy commandments; and yet thou never gavest me a kid, that I might make merry with my friends: But as soon as this thy son was come, which hath devoured thy living with harlots, thou hast killed for him the fatted calf. And he said unto him, Son, thou art ever with me and all that I have is thine. It was meet that we should make merry, and be glad: for this thy brother was dead, and is alive again; and was lost, and is found."

This is a story of the boy that did not go away from home. He does not care to claim kin with his prodigal brother, but he is close kin to him none the less. They are brothers not simply because they are sons of the same father. They are brothers in character. They are both self-seekers. They are both concerned, at least at the beginning of the story, with pleasing themselves,

with gaining their own ends rather than with pleasing
their father. Of the two, the one that stayed at home
is the more hopeless because he is less conscious of his
need. In fact, he has no sense of need at all. He believes himself an object of genuine congratulation.

I

Look at the story: "Now his elder son was in the
field." That is fine so far. That was where he belonged. He was out where the yellow wheat waved in
billows. He was out where the barley rustled and
spilled out its perfume. He was out where the blue
sky bent above him and the sun kissed a healthful tan
upon his cheeks. He was out where he could breathe an
atmosphere that was sweet and pure. He was where he
could avail himself of the strong moral support of a
wholesome environment. He was in the place of all
others where he had the best chance to keep clean. He
was in the field.

Not only so, but he had actually appropriated many
of the benefits of his fine environment. He had kept
clean. His garments might have a bit of the odour of
new-mown hay upon them, but they were certainly not
rank with the stench of the hog pen. He had never
visited the Far Country. He had never sowed any
wild oats. He had not marred and scarred himself by
long years of dissipation. He had remained thoroughly
decent. And all this is very commendable.

In addition, he was a worker. "Now his elder son
was in the field." That speaks of toil. There is sweat
in the word. There is the stern strain of effort. This
man is no idler. He is no parasite. He is an earnest
and strenuous worker. His prodigal brother does not

work with him. He has gone into the Far Country. He is wasting his substance with riotous living. But no waster is this elder brother. He is a toiler. And for this also we cannot but commend him.

II

And yet our Lord has not one good word to say about this elder son. What is the matter with him? Why does not Christ commend him? Was it wrong for him to be in the field? No, that is where he ought to have been. Was it wrong for him to work? No, work was his duty. Christ longs for every one to be a worker. He commands His disciples to pray the Lord of the harvest to thrust forth labourers into His harvest. The trouble with this elder son is not that he was in the field. It is not that he was a clean and decent worker. He is condemned rather because of the spirit in which he did his work.

Dr. Hubbard has aptly called this elder son a drudge. He is that most pathetic of all drudges—a religious drudge. What is drudgery? A mean task? No, drudgery is not the task, it is the spirit in which we perform the task. One man can make drudgery out of the singing of an anthem, while another can make poetry out of the scrubbing of a floor. To do your work in the spirit of loveless slavery is drudgery, however sublime the task may be at which you toil. On the other hand, if you work in the spirit of love, that work is shot through with abiding beauty, however ugly and menial your task may be in itself.

Here are two nurses that work in the same hospital. To one of them the task is purely professional. She watches, she gives medicine, she cools the fevered face.

She is capable, efficient, earnest, but all she sees is the
pay check at the end of the week. She is a drudge. But
the other: She too watches, toils, gives out her strength.
Possibly she is no more efficient than her sister. But
as she goes in and out among these sons and daughters
of pain, this song is in her heart:

> "Oh, how could I serve in the wards
> If the Hope of the World were a lie.
> How could I endure the sights
> And the loathsome smell of disease
> But that He said: 'Ye do it for me
> When ye do it for these!'"

And to this latter the task is no longer drudgery. It is
flooded with the radiant light that beams from the very
face of Christ.

Who is this man pegging away day after day on old
shoes? He is a cobbler. He is a drudging shoemaker.
His name is Carey. No, a cobbler he is, but not a
drudge. He is pegging shoes under the light of the
Sun of Righteousness. The song of his hammer is the
song that the angels sang above the star-lit heights of
Bethlehem. The vision that he sees reaches far beyond
the meagre sum he is to receive for his work. The
mending of those worn shoes is a means to a glorious
end. By his toil the feet of some that sit in darkness
are to be shod with the preparation of the Gospel of
peace. And here again what might have been drudgery is transformed into poetry by a beautiful motive.

But no such motive transfigured the work of this
elder son. There was no love in his task. He did not
care for this prodigal brother. Since he did not love
his wandering brother, he was equally destitute of love
for his father. For "if we love not our brother whom

we have seen, how can we love God whom we have not seen?" The measure of our love to God is what we are willing to do for men. Our devotion to the Unseen is read in our faithful and loyal devotion to those whom we see. It is impossible to love God and at the same time fail to love our brother.

III

Having no love for his brother, there was no pain at seeing him go away. He took the sin and the riotous living of the prodigal very little to heart. The fact that he was in the Far Country starving among swine did not worry this elder brother in the least. He never spent a sleepless night or a sleepless hour over the wrong doing of himself or of any one else. He did not care that men sinned. His father cared. His father grieved and broke his heart. But though his father might have wet his pillow with midnight tears, it mattered nothing to his loveless elder son.

Since this elder son did not share his father's grief over the loss of the prodigal, neither did he share his father's watchfulness for him. He had no part in his eager longing for his return. His father's face was ever toward the Far Country. He was always looking, always loving, always yearning. When at last the prodigal came home, "while he was yet a great way off his father saw him and ran and fell on his neck and kissed him." But this elder son did not see the returning wanderer. He refused to even meet him when he got home.

Not only did he fail to grieve over the wandering of the prodigal, not only did he fail to watch yearningly for his return, but when he came his coming brought

the elder brother no joy. "As he came and drew nigh
to the house, he heard music and dancing. And he
called one of the servants and asked what these things
meant. The servant said: Thy brother is come; and
thy father hath killed the fatted calf, because he hath
received him safe and sound. And he was angry and
would not go in." This marvellous event not only failed
to bring him joy, it brought him positive pain. It made
him angry.

Why was he angry? Not because his prodigal brother
had done him any harm. His anger was born of his
envy. This elder brother was envious. Therefore,
there was no joy in this occasion for him. All the music
was discord because it was not played in his honour
alone. The feast was altogether unpalatable because it
was not prepared solely for himself. He was possessed
of that hideous demon of envy, therefore any honour
done to another was a galling dishonour to himself.

Envy is an old sin. It committed the first crime that
was ever committed. The first murderous club that
was ever wielded was held by its devilish hand. It was
envy that murdered Abel. It was envy that sold Joseph
into slavery. It was envy that hurled the dart at David.
It was envy that plaited the crown of thorns for the
brow of our Lord. It was envy that nailed Him to the
cross. "He knew that for envy they had delivered Him
up."

What is envy? It is not to be confused with jealousy.
Jealousy, as another has pointed out, is a child of love.
When love is cheated of its dues, it has a right to be
jealous. There are times, I confess, when jealousy becomes "the green-eyed monster that makes the meat it
feeds upon." But oftentimes its meat is made for it.
When that is the case, jealousy is neither base nor ig-

noble. God is capable of jealousy. And the same may be said of all who really love.

Envy, on the other hand, is the child of hate. It has no connection with love whatsoever. We never envy those whom we truly love. "Love envieth not." Envy is that fiendish spirit that makes one feel uncomfortable when the ability, or attainment, or character of another is praised. It is a hellish serpent that stings us when we hear of the prosperity of a rival. I know a beautiful woman who seems to take it as almost a positive insult when some other woman's beauty is complimented. That is envy. It is a sin that few confess, but of which many are guilty. Ugly, cruel and devilish as it is, we hardly rid ourselves of it except by the grace of God.

IV

Notice next the experience of this drudge. He had remained at home. He had never gone into the Far Country. Therefore, we naturally expect that he will have a wonderful story to tell of blessed fellowship with his Father. We count upon it that he will be able to lead us to wonderful springs of which only those most intimate with his Father have knowledge. We expect him to be wise to bring us into marvellous gardens that the father has made known to him during his long sojourn at home. When he tells his experience, we lean eagerly forward. We feel sure of hearing a testimony at once winsome and inspiring.

But we are disappointed. This is his experience: "Lo, these many years do I serve thee, neither transgressed I at any time thy commandment; and yet thou never gavest me a kid that I might make merry with my friends." How astonishing! How disappointing! Did you ever hear a more pathetic testimony? "I have been serving my Father," says this man, "five years, ten years, twenty years, but it has meant absolutely nothing to me but hard work. There have been no glad surprises along the way. There have been no lovely oases. It has all been desert. Every day has been sunless and dull and drab and grey. I have lived in my Father's house, but I have lived not as a son, but as a slave. I have lived within reach of the Bread of Life, but I have never tasted it. I have lived with the song of the Water of Life sounding in my ears, but I have never stooped to drink."

Poor fellow! How completely he has missed everything that makes sonship beautiful and worth while! How utterly wanting he is in likeness to his Father! How wanting, therefore, in winsomeness! He reminds us of an artificial flower. What is wrong with that handsome rose? It is quite rose-like in its shape and colour. Yet there is something lacking. What? It has no life. It has never mined in the rich loam of the garden for the gold of real beauty. It has never been christened by the gentle baptism of the rain. It has never drunk from the mystic chalice of the dew. It has never had its cheek touched by the sun's magic brush. It has a form of life without the reality. And so it was with this toiling drudge. He has a form of sonship, but the winsome reality is not his.

And, sad to say, this elder son is not in a class to himself. There are literally hundreds and thousands who, if they spoke the honest truth, would have to confess that their religious lives had been disappointing. They have not found in the Church of Christ what they expected to find. A woman who was a member of my church said some time ago that before she came into

the Church she thought it was going to mean so much.
And then she sighed and said: "But I have found that
it means very little. I am just like I was before I
joined."

Why is this the case? Is it because Christ cannot
do what He claims to do? Is it because this Word of
God is only a cunningly devised fable? Whose fault
was it that this elder son had such a lean and mean experience? Whose fault was it that his life had been
such a disappointment to himself and such a disappointment to his Father? Our Lord indicates the
reason. What said the Father to the son when he com-
plained that he had never given him so much as a kid
with which to make merry with his friends? He did
not deny the charge. He virtually admits that the son
is correct. But the reason he had given him nothing
was because he was not willing to receive it.

V

Look at the privileges that might have been his.
"Son, thou art ever with me, and all that I have is
thine." This son of his might have had continuous fellowship with his Father. That is the experience to
which God longs to bring every child of His. He ever
yearns to make His promise, "Lo, I am with you
alway" an actual experience with every one of us.
There is absolutely nothing for which He is so eager as
our companionship. He wants to be with us in our joys
and in our sorrows. He wants to be with us in life's
springtime, and also in life's winter.

And what do we need so much as this divine companionship? How we need Christ in our hours of tempta-
tion! I knew a young man who years ago was con-

verted from a life of dissipation. For a while he was an earnest and devout Christian. But in an hour of weakness he fell. He was so ashamed of his fall that he hid himself from his faithful pastor. But that pastor sought him and found him and fought with him for his soul. At last he won him back to loyalty to Christ. Years passed on and that rescued man entered the ministry. One day as he and his one-time pastor were walking together to the church, this reclaimed man told of his constant battle with the sin that had almost wrought his ruin years ago. Then he paid this pastor a great tribute. He said: "You know I feel that I would never be tempted after this fashion if I always had you with me." But his friend replied: "I am not what you need. What you need is Jesus. You can have Him with you always, even to the end."

"Son, thou art ever with me." How we need Jesus in our hours of sorrow! How we need Him when hearts are broken and our hopes shattered! He can bring light to us when all is utter darkness. He can companion us and understand us and comfort us when all human help fails. You may recall that old story of Florence Nightingale, "the Angel of the Crimea": A wounded soldier had to undergo a severe operation. His heart would not permit his taking an anæsthetic. So the doctor informed him that he had better not operate since the pain would be so great that he could not endure it. But the soldier replied that he could endure it under one condition. "I can bear the pain if you will get the Angel of the Crimea to hold my hand during the operation." And this fine saint of God took the rough soldier's hand in her own and held it and caressed it as his mother might. And the knife cut through the tender flesh, and the saw cut through the

bone, and the soldier never flinched. When the operation was over the doctor said in amazement, "I do not
see how you stood it." But he answered: "I could not
do otherwise. My hand was in the hand of the Angel
of the Crimea." So in these painful experiences of
life that cut into our very hearts, it is our privilege to
have our hands, not in some weak human hand, but in
the hand of the mighty Christ.

Not only was it the privilege of this elder son to have
had the constant fellowship of his Father, but he might
have possessed all his Father's wealth. Listen! "All
that I have is thine." And that same word our Lord
is speaking to our poverty-stricken hearts. "All things
are yours." And is there anything more tragic than
just this: That we are spiritually poor when we might
be rich; that we are weak when we might be strong;
that we are defeated and overcome when we might be
conquerors? "All that I have is thine." Infinitely
more eager than we are to receive is He to give.

It is said that when Helen Keller, that deaf, dumb
and blind genius, was a baby, her mother used to bend
over her as she lay in the cradle and drop her hot tears
down upon her. And she would speak after this fashion:
"Oh, Helen, how your mother loves you! And how she
longs to tell you of her love! But she cannot make you
understand. Your eyes are closed and your ears are
stopped." It was the heartache of this mother that she
longed to reveal herself; that she longed to give herself
unreservedly to her child, and yet could not make her
understand.

So this father was feeling toward his elder son. So
God feels toward His children always. He is bending
very wistfully above you and me to-day. And He is
saying: "Oh, child of my heart, how I love you! And

how I long to give you of my very best! How I long
to enrich you with all spiritual gifts! How I long to
bring you to your highest possibilities! 'All things are
yours.' 'Son, thou art ever with me, and all that I have
is thine.' " Let us claim what the heavenly Father so
longs to give. Heaven's best may be ours. "He that
spared not His own Son, but delivered Him up for us
all, how shall He not with Him also freely give us all
things." And thus receiving, life's drudgery will be
changed into winsome poetry.

XVI

THE DYING FIRE—TIMOTHY

II Timothy 1:16

"Stir up the gift that is within thee."

I

The word here translated "stir up" really means re-kindle. "My dear Timothy," wrote Paul. "Knowing as I do the trying circumstances in which you are placed, I realise that you are in great danger of losing your zeal. I realise how greatly you are tempted to allow the fires of your enthusiasm to go out. There-fore, I write you this word, Rekindle the gift of God that is within you. Look well to your fire lest it burn low and utterly die."

You can see that Paul is not accusing Timothy of having put out his own fire. He did not say, "Stop throwing water on the fire of your zeal." In order for a fire to go out it is not necessary always that it be put out. When you light the fire in the furnace all you have to do to lose that fire and let winter invade your home is simply to let it alone. And all that is neces-sary in order for you to waste your gifts, to let all that God has invested in you go for nothing, is simply to let those gifts alone.

Paul is not accusing Timothy of misusing his gifts. He is not afraid that he is taking the talents that God has given him and turning them to base and ignoble uses. Some people waste their substance with riotous living. Others waste theirs with quite respectable and quite decent living. In the Far Country by the swine trough is not the only place where men squander their abilities. They are often squandered no less by people who occupy pews in churches. They are squandered by those who are well-wishers of the Church and of all the forces that make for the world's upbuilding, but who do nothing but wish.

Nor is Paul urging Timothy to acquire new gifts. He is not urging him to use gifts that he does not possess. He simply presses home upon him the sane and practical duty of using what he actually has. "Stir up the gift that is within thee." It is not necessary for you to sing with the voice of another or to preach with the power of another. Your whole duty is to minister with your own hands, walk on errands of mercy upon your own feet, speak, as God has given you power, through your own lips. Use the gift that God has committed to you. That is your duty and your whole duty. And that is all that is necessary for the bringing in of the Kingdom of God.

If we were only as willing to use our own gifts as we fancy we should be to use the gifts of others, what a different Church we should have and what a different world this would be! We know quite well what it is to wish that we were as gifted as certain other individuals. If we were only as rich as a certain man we know, how much we would give! If we could only sing like a friend of ours, how constantly we would use our powers to the glory of God! But God's question to us is His question to Moses: "What is that in thy hand?" He is not concerned with what we do with the gifts of another. He is only concerned with what we do with our own. If He can get what we ourselves actually possess, if He can bring us by any persuasion to the full dedication of our own powers to Him, then His purpose in our lives has been realised.

II

To whom is Paul writing this urgent appeal?

1. He is writing to a Christian. He is not writing to a heathen. He is not writing to one who utterly ignores Christ and His Church. He is writing to a young man of whose conversion he has no doubt. In fact it was Paul's privilege to lead this young man into a knowledge of Jesus Christ. Timothy was his son in the Gospel and Paul loved him with the passionate devotion of a mother. It is with deep joy that he calls to remembrance the unfeigned faith that is in Timothy. He does not doubt in the least this young man's loyalty to Christ. And yet he finds it necessary to urge upon him the necessity of rekindling his fire.

2. Not only is Paul writing to a Christian, but he is writing to a Christian minister. He had been called, Paul reminds him, with a holy calling. He had known by experience the glad thrill of being a herald of the unsearchable riches of Christ. Timothy was a preacher. He was engaged in the highest of all tasks. He was occupied with the most fascinating of all labours. And yet even to this man Paul writes this urgent word: "Stir up the gift that is within thee."

III

Why did Timothy need this exhortation from Paul?

1. He needed it because he was in a hard situation.

There is never a time when Christian work is altogether easy. Let us face the fact at once that the carrying on of Christ's work in the world always has meant and always will mean struggle and conflict. It is hard to stand for Christ to-day if you stand for Him truly. It was exceedingly hard in the day in which Timothy lived. Christians were very few. To go forth as a disciple of Jesus Christ was to be in a small minority. But there was far more involved than this. It was to be scorned, to be hated, to be persecuted, to be imprisoned, oftentimes to be put to death. Thus Timothy, separated from his father in the Gospel, needed this heartening message lest, under the pressure of difficulties, he should allow his gifts to go to waste.

2. He needed this message because of his extreme youth. Timothy had never succeeded in growing up. He never could get to the place where he was impressive to look at. He was not so fortunate as some in that direction. People could easily ignore him because he seemed such a youth. But Timothy was a preacher. He had, therefore, of necessity to take some part of leadership. But how hard it was when people were always saying, as we would say to-day, "What a kid!" So much was this the case that Paul had to urge upon him not to let his youthfulness impair his usefulness. "Let no man despise thy youth," he writes. Timothy was in danger of simply dropping to the rear of the procession and saying, "Let those who are older carry on the work." God needs the old folks, but He also needs the youth. Therefore, to the young, as well as to the old, He says: "Stir up the gift that is within thee."

3. Then Timothy needed this exhortation because he was timid. Now, there are those who simply laugh at

timidity. But those who have known the agonies of it
are not disposed to laugh. There are some people who
do not know what it is to be timid. But there are
others who are altogether different. They become un-
nerved at the very thought of appearing before an audience. They turn hot and cold at the mere suggestion of
their taking any public part in Christian work.
Timothy was such a man. He knew what it was to
become quite as confused over the handling of his shaky
knees as he did over the handling of his sermon.

On one occasion Paul sends this timid young preacher
on a mission to Corinth. The great apostle knows that
his son in the Gospel is going to have a hard time. It
is easy to read between the lines how Paul's heart fairly
bleeds for him. As he sees him off he gives him all the
encouragement possible. He reminds him of his constant prayers for him. He reminds him also that he has
written a personal letter to the Church at Corinth urging them to receive him kindly. "If Timothy come,"
he wrote, "see that he be with you without fear." "Be
gentle with him," he seems to say. "He is very timid.
Hold him up by your prayers and your sympathy.
Make it as easy for him as you can. If you are disposed
to be too critical of him, I fear you will frighten him
out of the ministry altogether."

4. Timothy needed this exhortation because he was
physically weak. Timothy was not a man of robust
and vigorous body. He was subject to sick spells that
left his cheeks pale and his limbs a-tremble and his energies depleted. He had an affliction of the stomach that
laid him low again and again. And because it is hard
to work when pain is constantly nagging at you, because it is hard to stick to your task when disease is
thrusting you again and again with its sword, Paul

thought wise to urge upon Timothy the necessity of
stirring up the gift of God that was within him.

Now, far be it from me to speak lightly of the heroic
knights of the sick-room. Far be·it from me to mini-
mise the pain of those whose every hour is a
fisticuff with some tormenting malady. But I would
remind you that often we allow a slight sickness to keep
us from doing our religious duties, when that same
sickness would not interfere with us in the least in a
matter of business or in a matter of pleasure. I would
remind you further that some of the mightiest victories
for God have been won by those whose lives were one
long battle with physical disease.

You see that man limping his way to his task like one
who has been sore wounded in the battle. He is
wounded. He has been thrust through with a thorn.
And that thorn no surgeon has been able to remove. It
is still there jabbing at him as if in fiendish glee. It is
constantly torturing him as if in sheer malice. In con-
sequence of his painful wounds he groans and bleeds in
the day and groans and bleeds in the night. But he
goes on with his work. Yea, the time comes when his
work seems even more effective because of his infirmities. God has spoken to him and said: "My grace is
sufficient for thee. My strength is made perfect in
weakness." And hear his answer: "Therefore, I take
pleasure in infirmities, in reproaches, in necessities, in
persecutions, in distresses for Christ's sake: for when I
am weak, then am I strong."

As I walked the streets of Edinburgh not long ago, I
thought of another weak-bodied hero, Robert Louis Ste-
venson. Whenever he took his pen to write, sickness
sat close beside him. Fever flushed his cheek and made
his heart beat fast. And how dry his lips became, and

his head, how it ached! But still he worked and still
he smiled and still he helped. He never ceased as long
as life was in him to stir up his gift. A great courageous soul labouring in a tottering house. How like
him this work from his own pen:

"Under the broad and starry sky
Dig me a grave and let me lie;
Glad did I live and gladly die,
And I laid me down with a will."

IV

What reason does Paul urge upon Timothy for stirring up his gift?

He does not ask him to stir up the gift that is within
him because of any great financial return that is coming to him. He does not urge upon him this duty and
give as a reason that he will thus be able to fill some
great city pulpit. Paul himself had preached in these
great cities, but his pulpit had at times been a whip-
ping post and at other times a prison cell. He did not
urge this duty upon Timothy because the task was becoming easier and opposition was altogether melting
away. He offers absolutely no reason that would appeal
to Timothy's personal ambition or cater in the least to
his cowardice.

1. There is great need on account of great opposition. "Evil men and seducers," Paul says, "are going
to wax worse and worse. There are those already, and
their number will increase, that have itching ears, and
they will turn away their ears from the truth and give
heed unto fables." He declares further that the time
will come when many will have only a form of Godli

ness without the power. They will cling to the husk and let the grain go. They will grasp at the shadow and fling away the substance.

"Now, Timothy," Paul writes, "since evil days are ahead of us, since you are quite likely to be called to serve churches many among whose membership will have itching ears, you must be prepared to act accordingly. Since you will quite likely have among your hearers those who have only a form of Godliness without the power, and since these are going to oppose your spiritual preaching and make your task exceedingly difficult, I advise that you give over the ministry and cease toiling at so hopeless an undertaking as the bringing in of the Kingdom." That would have been a natural bit of advice, but it is not what Paul says. He rather tells his young friend that, inasmuch as there are many dangers and much opposition ahead, it is highly important that he stir up the gift of God that is within him.

What effect does opposition have upon you? How do you feel toward a hard and trying and discouraging situation? The church in your neighbourhood—is it full of spiritual power, or is it a chilly and sleepy and icebound affair? Supposing that it is, will you withdraw? You will never cure it that way. Nobody helps by quitting. "Behold, I stand at the door and knock," said Jesus. "If any man will open the door and come out I will sup with him." Did I quote that right? I have quoted it the way many people seem to read it. There are tens and thousands that are letting the churches absolutely alone to-day, giving as their reason that they are so dead, so far behind the times, so useless. But Jesus did not invite us to quit. He said: "If any man will open the door, I will come in." The need of this hour is not for more folks to get out of the Church. It is for more of us to open the door and let Christ into the Church. And the greater the deadness of your church, the greater the need. And the greater the need, the more urgent the call for you to "stir up the gift that is within thee."

2. Paul urges Timothy to stir up his gift for the sake of his personal salvation. In giving himself to his task, in utilising his gift to the utmost, Paul said that Timothy would save himself. Now I do not take it that this is one of the many ways of salvation. If Timothy will not use his gifts he will lose them and lose himself as well. If Jesus Christ emphasised any one fact above all others, it was the fact that to simply keep hands off, to do nothing, is the sin of all sins. Every parable of judgment that He uttered, so far as I have been able to find out, is a parable pronounced because of a service withheld.

3. The final reason that Paul gives Timothy for investing his entire self in his task goes beyond the promise that he will save himself by so doing. The salvation of self may seem to you an unworthy motive. Then, take the next one. He said: "By so doing, you will both save yourself and them, that hear you." Timothy had it in his power to be a blessing to the needy churches of his day and to the needy men and women of his day. He had it in his power to be a blessing through all the long centuries. And you have it in your power, by putting your gifts in God's hands, to save not only yourself, but to save other precious lives that are even dearer to you than your own.

v

How did Timothy treat this urgent word from St. Paul? He responded. He stirred up his gift. Paul could still write to him as he had written in earlier days: "He works the work of God, as I also do." Timothy is very timid, is he not? Yes, but he works. Is not Timothy an exceedingly young man? Yes, but he is a worker. Is that Timothy coughing? He is sick, is he not? Quite sick. Pain seems to play with him constantly, yet Timothy works. They laughed at Timothy when he tried to preach. Yes, but he did not quit. Timothy went on working.

Then one day they brought him this letter. As he read it his hands trembled—his thin, weak hands. And his cheeks, usually pale, became flushed. And big tears ran down his face till he could hardly make out the words on the parchment: "Dear Timothy: I have the sadness to inform you that all those in Asia have turned away from me. At present I am in prison in Rome. 'Demas hath forsaken me, having loved this present world.' I had a hearing before Cæsar recently, but at the trial no man stood with me. I was utterly alone. Come to me. Do your best to come before winter."

And what did this sickly, timid, youthful preacher do? He said: "Well, poor Paul. I would like to be with him to help him the best I could, but it is a long journey and I feel so bad. He is in prison too, and if I go I too am likely to get into prison. In my present state of health I think prison life would prove the death of me. I cannot go." No, that is not Timothy's response. He took his fears in his frail hands and strangled them. And when Paul went to the block there were at least two friends with him. One of them was Luke, the beloved physician, brave, gentle Luke. And the other was Timothy, timid, shy, retiring, sickly Timothy.

I wonder what it would have been like to have seen this meeting between Paul and Timothy. How the white-haired old man rejoiced over his coming! He was glad to see him because he was lonesome. But there was a far deeper gladness than that. It was the joy he had in Timothy's victory over his own fears. His heart was singing like the strings of a violin touched by a master because Timothy was really stirring up the gift that was within him.

VI

How did Timothy win his fight?

1. He had much human help. Grandmother Lois was praying for him, no doubt. And beside her in the secret place was his mother, Eunice. Then there was the abiding memory of Paul, his father in the faith. And then maybe some obscure saint whose name is not known here, but is most familiar in heaven, maybe this obscure saint helped him. I recall one such that I had in my congregation the first year of my ministry. More than once, when the load was heavy and the skies were black and the young preacher did not see how he could get through the service, did this sweet saint of God come to his assistance. To this day I feel the pressure of his arm about me. To this day I hear the whisper of his voice: "God bless you," he would say, "God bless you. I am holding you up to-day. I am remembering you at the Throne of Grace." And strength came into my heart as tides come in from the sea.

2. Above all else Timothy owed his victory to Jesus Christ Himself. In spite of weakness and timidity he dared put himself in the hands of his Lord. For His sake he ventured to stir up his gifts. And as he thus obeyed God a new power came into his life, even the power of the Holy Spirit. "For we are witnesses of these things, and so is also the Holy Spirit whom God has given to those that obey Him." And His coming always makes for a new power and a Christlike courage. "They were all filled with the Holy Spirit, and they spoke the Word of God with boldness." Thus timid Timothy became a blessing to his day and to all future centuries. Thus we too may win if we will for Christ's sake stir up the gift that is within us.

THE END